Our Lost or Stolen Political Economic System

We are left with a greed powered utopia for a few

Charles B. Parker

ISBN: 1514349167
ISBN 13: 9781514349168
Library of Congress Control Number: 2015909839
CreateSpace Independent Publishing Platform
North Charleston, South Carolina

OUR POLITICAL ECONOMIC SYSTEM

We now have a greed-powered utopia
for a few.

When the problem is understood, the solution becomes
obvious, but very difficult.

Why?

The changes required mean changing

Us.

Our Lost Political Economic System

Introduction

When studying the forest,
make sure the trees don't block the view.

• • •

WHEN WE SEE the words *political* and *economy*, most of us immediately lose interest. We are confused because we read books or articles on the subject of the two words; or we listen to people on television, on the radio, or in meetings, during which one person's ideas on politics and economics conflict with other people's ideas. We often conclude that they are all trying to advance some self-interest, thus we believe the strategy of confusion is intended. Studying political economics is difficult because there are many different issues, subsystems, conflicting theories, political beliefs, and arrays of self-interest and greed that are involved; therefore, our not seeing the forest for the trees is understandable.

Making sense of the subject is possible, if we look at the historical basis of the subject rather than all the complexities that have been added primarily to serve self-interest. Adam Smith, the eighteenth-century Scottish political economic historian, recognized this problem when he studied and described the political economic system of fair capitalism, the system that was used in some parts of Europe at the time. His two texts published in 1759 and 1776 were the major political economic books in use during the establishment of the United States. Our founders properly considered Smith's data during the development of the Constitution and its political economic processes. Since then, there have been many misstatements of Smith's ideas that have influenced our legal and economic structure, one being the claim that Smith taught that greed was the essential motivator for economic growth in capitalism. He did not.

The purpose of this book is to tie all the basic elements of the subject together to give the reader a clear view of the forest. In the past this sort of study has been assisted by listing many references that a person can refer to; however, we now have the huge reference library of the Internet available, making it possible for readers to quickly look up information without having to deal with the possibility that the choice of references was influenced by the prejudices of the author. Please keep your computer, digital pad, or smartphone handy to use whenever you have questions. Most importantly, please keep your sixth sense in place to filter out the inevitable propaganda.

It has been traditional to discuss political economics in the language and literary form of the most learned in our society. The language and literary form used in this book will be familiar to most of us, but it may bring complaints from those who are professionals on the subject. They are concerned that, by not using complex professional terminology and language, the intellect of the average reader is devalued; however, that has not been the intention. The attempt has been to present the material in a factual, logical, interesting, and understandable form that will leave the reader with a positive and hopeful outlook for the future of our society.

THE PREAMBLE
TO THE CONSTITUTION

These are the principles upon which the Constitution is based.

We the People of the United States, in order to form a more perfect union, establish justice, insure domestic Tranquility, provide for a common defense, promote the general Welfare, and secure the Blessings of Liberty to ourselves and to our Posterity, do ordain and establish this Constitution for the United States of America.

Contents

1

Historical Introduction to Political Economics

"Study the past, if you would divine
the future."

—Confucius

THE STORY THAT becomes clear from the study of archaeology and history is that for the last hundred thousand years, humans have been searching for a society that will allow people to live together happily without killing each other. There have been short-term successes in small portions of the world, but little that can be considered a lasting success. The science of archaeology tells us that some societies functioned well, at least for a while, but something always destroyed the good ones.

Archaeologists also teach that four thousand years ago, the inhabitants of North Africa (in what is now Egypt and Sudan) developed the first society that could be called a state, and a monarch probably ruled it. This was the case with most states or societies over the next several thousand years. Two and a half thousand years ago, the Romans established the first republic where the people had the power rather than having the power concentrated in a monarch. While planning their society, they identified a number of reasons that past societies had failed, but the greatest cause of failure was the concentration of power in a few people or one person without a practical ability of the people to withdraw that power. The written history of that first hundred years of the Roman Republic is only partially reliable, but the objective was to completely control concentration of power by having two leaders with equal power. These leaders were changed after short terms, on an alternating basis from a pool of citizens who were educated, so that a single person of power could not develop. This apparently worked well to prevent power concentration for about one hundred years. Over the next five hundred years, the republican idea degenerated and the people lost their power. By about 50 BCE, Julius Caesar had complete power, and the republic was dissolved.

Historians have suggested many reasons for the failure of the Roman Republic, but the basic reason was that while conditions changed, the design of the republic didn't. The elite citizens who were responsible for maintaining the country's republican structure grew more interested in the great wealth that was streaming into Rome than maintaining the flexibility of their societal experiment and making adjustments for these changing conditions.

There is an interesting comparison between Rome's attempt to build a society based on the power of the people and our American experiment in building the same sort of society. The Romans stopped paying attention, that is, stopped making adjustments and corrections to the structure of their society because other interests began to dominate their thinking. One of those interests, according to many students of the Roman society, was spectator sports, which were mainly held in the Coliseum. Hopefully this doesn't apply to us.

The Greek democracy was established about the same time that the Roman Republic was in power. The design of that democracy has been a template for the design of many governments since then, but it required so much from its citizens that people soon tired, and the society went back to a concentrated power structure. Since then, many states with comingled political and economic structures were developed. Unfortunately, most didn't use the lessons learned from the earlier Greeks and Romans, so most had centralized power structures that were unjust. It is apparent that the lesson from these earlier societies is that the development of a society's political and economic system is a work in progress, an experiment that must be closely monitored and corrected for injustices that occur. It is also apparent that these injustices are brought about by the concentration of power and by the special interests of those persons in power.

In his first book in 1759, Adam Smith, wrote: "By acting according to the dictates of our moral facilities, we necessarily pursue the most effective means for promoting the happiness of mankind." Smith later wrote in 1776, "unbridled self-interest can also produce great harm to the common good," which was "the gifts of nature, of air, water, land and sea." He expanded this thinking in other ways that advanced the idea of the purpose of a political economic system of a society: to preserve the well-being of all living things and the planet. Much of Smith's philosophical thinking still applies to the conditions of our time, although some of his writings require an understanding of the language and culture of Scotland, his home.

The leaders of the North American colonies used some of Smith's ideas as well as the lessons of history to design and establish a *more perfect* state, the United States of America. The government they designed was based on the principle that power would be entirely with the people, and if the people remained responsible and vigilant, then the concentration of power would be prevented. The idea that citizens needed to be responsible and vigilant to protect a just society has been a pillar in the development of societies for thousands of years, but there has yet to be a society where citizens have continued serving that responsibility.

The founders of the United States of America of America also knew that concentration of wealth and concentration of power are almost the same. This means that economics can control the political structure, unless strong rules based on the principles of the Constitution become laws of the land. The rules need to be effective in controlling concentration of power through violence or wealth, and be based on the constitutional principle of justice., Greed commonly leads to injustice, so rules limiting greed are also necessary. Rules have not been continuously monitored and updated causing them to become less effective. As result, we have had times of severe injustice and, especially, economic injustice. It is important to remember that history gives evidence for what not to do, but since conditions continually change, history shouldn't be used as an absolute basis for what to do, .

I was born a few years before the Great Depression, which started in 1929 and didn't completely end until the Second World War brought the country to full employment. It was a decade that caused suffering for many and even death for some. Children during the Depression listened to adults discuss the causes of poverty and economic turmoil that most of them were enduring. It was the universal belief that the basic cause was greed—greed for wealth and power. People experiencing the Depression were concerned that the powerful people in the country had accepted the philosophy that *greed is good*; they felt that greed is the only true motivator, the only true driver of human progress. The *greed is good* philosophy has even been adopted by some who are religious, but most religions teach that love of others is good and greed is a sin. The early scholars in the Christian Church, working to record the teachings of Jesus before they were lost, placed greed as a major sin among the Seven Deadly Sins.

When looked at carefully, our country's principle of justice—based on fair rules—is the opposite of the principle of greed, and it is our duty to make sure our leaders and rule makers understand that. People living during those early Depression years, and especially those with some education in history, discussed economics and government with extreme interest. They were sensitive to the fact that the proper functioning of society was their responsibility. The young people had the rules of economics and the Constitution drilled into them, along with the religion-based rules spelling out the differences between love, hate, and greed. Those who were children at that time were fortunate because these basic rules were vividly meaningful, as they were living during the best time to learn about these things—the Great Depression. Most of those who were children during the Great Depression have gone through life being strongly motivated to guard against thinking and activities that could damage their society by causing it to become greed based.

Those who lived through the Great Depression and war years are thankful that the principles that have made this a just society were hammered into a constitution during the last decade of the eighteenth century, after years of serious debate. However, not all the delegates to the Constitutional Convention agreed with the principles contained in the final document, and a number of them didn't sign it. As with much legislation in the present day, compromises had to be made in some principles in order to have a majority adopt the Constitution. Southern delegates wanted to keep the rights of the state governments much stronger than the rights of the federal government because they wanted to keep the state right of slavery. Keeping the Union a weaker confederation of states would protect that right. Another powerful force against a strong federal constitution came from many of the landed gentry from both the North and South. They felt that their power would be protected if the states, where they had great power, remained stronger than the federal government. This meant that there were many at the Constitutional Convention who felt strongly that the new country should not be a true republic where every citizen had an equal power to that of every other citizen in the entire country. Those delegates to the convention that were against strong federal government became known as Anti-Federalists. The Anti-Federalists actually prevailed in a major way. The Senate, which has great power in Congress, was not chosen by equal vote of the people. Two senators from each state were to be appointed by the respective legislature of a state. Since the populations of the states were very unequal, the citizens' power to choose senators was unequal.

The Federalists felt passionately that the Union could only survive with a strong federal government. Interestingly, most of the members who considered themselves to be Federalists were also members of the landed gentry who put the good of the Union ahead of their personal power. The main argument for strong federal power was that without it, there would be no way to settle serious disagreements between the states, and these disagreements could even end in wars between the states. This was disastrously demonstrated when the compromise allowing slavery weakened the principle of justice, resulting in the Civil War. These compromises reducing the federal power produced many situations when state power was superior to federal power, which in some cases was good, but there have been many disagreements that have been impossible to settle.

The Federalists believed that the Constitution established a republic that gave the power to *We the People*, which means all of the people. Therefore, a person in any state had power equal to a person in any other state. There is also an unwritten rule in our society that the feelings and needs of minorities should not be ignored, but these feelings and needs should not take a strong precedence over the needs of the majority of all the people.

The one extremely important principle our Union has made clear, but many of us haven't accepted, is that a strong Union—rather than a group of semi-independent states—is the glue that has made possible the successful development of our great nation. If those few American states had been left semi-independent, it is obvious that chaos would have eventually destroyed the work of our founders. Now, two hundred years later, the entire world is in the same situation that those states were in during the late 1700s. Now the world has its version of the landed gentry in each nation-state, which makes it difficult to consider a truly international union of countries. The people of the United States have worked on making our Union more perfect with much success. A world union based on the principle of justice would likely take one hundred years to become organized and much longer to reach the more perfect stage that the United States has reached. The world was ready to start such a union with the League of Nations after the First World War, but the extreme national-ism that has been a pattern throughout history ended that try. The United Nations started with great hope after the Second World War, but it may never become a union because leaders of several great world powers will never accept not being entirely interdependent. However, a World Court was generally accepted even though the United States would not agree to join. Apparently, we must wait for new generations to end the carnage of war, or—if we don't—we may be destined to return to a Stone Age–type of civilization.

Several years ago there was a discussion group of men and women at a university reunion; the discussed subject turned to the meaning and importance of their lives. All had lived through the Great Depression as children, and most were veterans of the Second World War. Much of their education had been paid through the GI Bill—the veterans' education program that made it possible for many of them to become part of what is known as the Greatest Generation. This is the generation credited by many as the generation that used its education and dedication to rebuild America following the Great Depression and the Second World War.

The reunion discussion was enthusiastic and ended with the group agreeing that the reason their generation was able to do great things was their motivation to transform their nation and the world into a place where justice and the pursuit of happiness would dominate. They were driven to do their best to make sure that the terrible things that they had witnessed during the Depression and the war would never again happen. They were confident when they finished their education that, besides rebuilding America, they would be able to raise and educate their family, have a good standard of living, and have a reasonable retirement. The group was made up of both Republicans and Democrats that were very pleased with the functioning of the government during the war and for a few years after. The Marshall Plan for Europe, the national highway program, the general infrastructure improvements, the communication system, and many other efforts were things to which they had been proudly dedicated.

The period when people strongly desired to build structures and institutions that would benefit the country while providing them with a good, safe, and happy life lasted for about twenty-five years after the end of the war. There was some international strife during that time, which people believed was caused by their failure to heed the warning from their war hero, President Dwight Eisenhower. He warned that by allowing what he called the military-industrial complex to control the country's international relations and domestic policies would lead to diminished national greatness. The evidence that this advice was being ignored became strong in the 1970s and 1980s, when it was clear that national actions were based more on the desire to build an infrastructure used to create an industrial and military world power rather than on the real needs of national security. Unfortunately, ignoring that advice resulted in the fulfillment of President Eisenhower's fears with the near-universal belief that the greed for wealth and power was the only motivator that would bring great benefits to society.

The members of the university discussion group were ordinary people, like you or possibly your parents or grandparents, who lived through that time and saw the rebuilding happen with their eyes; therefore, it has been hard to deceive them. The group agreed that it was necessary for the general public to understand the true history of how this all came about and especially the political economic component, because they were there to witness it. Surely, these types of discussions have happened many times in similar groups that lived in such times, by those who were part of a generation with similarly expressed feelings. This gives good evidence that the primary motivator for improvement of our society is not greed, but rather a desire to work with others for improvement; and as a result, each person's desire for healthy self-interest would be fulfilled.

2

Economics and the Constitution

These are the first seventeen words of the Constitution: "We the People of the United States, in Order to form a more perfect Union, establish Justice..."

THOUSANDS OF YEARS ago, humanity began to move away from the hunter-gatherer system of survival to systems that could maintain a larger population. This was characterized by the long process known in history as the *division of labor*, which was the starting point for the development of all societies. This was due to the early understanding that humans working as a team could more efficiently guarantee their survival. It was also discovered that a team could avoid moving into dysfunction only by having rules of fairness; the problem of developing fair rules has plagued teams and societies over the millennia.

Working as a team with rules of fairness is the basic definition of a game, so what we are talking about is essentially the game of society. There are two problems with the rules of games that can cause such games to disintegrate. A part of the study of physics is the study of complexity, which states that you can never accurately predict the outcome of actions of complex systems. Complex systems are systems containing more than three variables. Games are complex systems. This means that you can never make a rule that will permanently ensure fairness in a game; therefore, you cannot predict accurately the outcome over time. The second problem is that humans will attempt to use rules in an unfair way or change rules unfairly over time, so that fairness is lost. This means that no hard-and-fast rule can guarantee fairness or justice—two words that mean the same thing—over time because justice is a *moving target*, and the rules to protect justice need to be flexible and variable. Developing a good set of rules was what the Constitutional Convention worked to create.

It is helpful to understand the mood of those assembled in the Constitution Hall in Philadelphia that early summer of 1787. The room was small, much too small for the number of people assembled, and it was, of course, not air-conditioned. The clothing was ornate and bulky, and it was patterned after the clothing worn by the gentry of Europe. Some wore wigs. Under those conditions it was understandable that tempers were very short, and the discourse was often so intense that it made our present disagreements in Congress seem like small talk. The group's objective when they arrived at the hall in Philadelphia was to revise the Articles of Confederation, the original governing document for the new country. After attempting to make reasonable revisions, the assembly decided that an entirely new constitution would be necessary, and after less than two months, the new constitution was approved by a majority of the assembly. It is hard to believe that in such an atmosphere, a document with such unifying principles and workable structure could be conceived.

The developers of our US Constitution, with much of the primary work done by James Madison and Alexander Hamilton, carefully considered the problems in developing a *more perfect* society. They realized, when looking at the evidence of many millennia of history, that a perfect society was impossible. We know they solved that problem by using the term *more perfect* in the development of the rules of society they were attempting to establish, since *more perfect* means closer to perfect. It was another stroke of genius when they decided to write the book of rules, the Constitution, in two distinct parts. The first part, called the preamble, is a statement of hard-and-fast, almost cast in stone, principles. The word *preamble* has caused confusion in understanding the importance of that statement. Possibly, the words *statement of principles* would have been a better heading. These principles were to be basic to our new society and were to be extremely difficult or impossible to change. The second part, the body of the Constitution, was a structure designed to implement and to carry out the principles set forth in the first part. The body of the Constitution was meant to be changeable as the conditions and definitions of justice changed, but these changes were to take place only after very careful consideration. The Constitution also provides for a system to make just laws. Laws would be easier to change if laws were shown to be unjust as conditions changed.

The preamble, containing the principles upon which the Constitution is based, consists of only one sentence, but it states the principles that are the foundation of our society. The text "We the People" states that the power belongs to the people, but establishing this principle during the heated debate in the Constitutional Convention of 1787 was not easy. Many, possibly a majority, felt that the people were not capable of being given this responsibility. Many of the people could neither read nor write and had very little education. It was finally agreed that this problem could be solved by establishing a universal education system and by giving special responsibility to the press for keeping the people accurately informed. This established the principle, not completely stated in the Constitution, that an *informed and vigilant* citizenry would, under the Constitution, maintain a stable society.

The fifteenth word in the Constitution is *Union*. This word could now be changed to society, but the word *Union* was extremely important at the time because it was strongly felt that we needed to avoid the wars produced by the many countries of the world that had no unifying government to settle disagreements. Much of the fighting during the convention was centered on the disagreement between those believing we should have very strong state governments and a weak central government, and those believing we should have a strong union with a strong central government. This fight resulted in the formation of two groups, the Federalists and the Anti-Federalists. This fight continues to this day with states' rights groups believing that the Anti-Federalists' opinions had prevailed in the meaning of the Constitution. Those of modern federalist thinking feel that states rights need to be subdued but not eliminated after the disaster of having to settle the assumed state right of slavery during the Civil War. Federalist thinkers believe that no assumed state right can violate any principle set forth in the principles section of the Constitution, including the principle of the right to justice.

The Federalists were concerned that if the states had power greater than the federal government, they could do such things as have armies, which could result in wars. The Anti-Federalists, who were represented to a great extent by the powerful landed gentry of the states, were concerned that their power would be lost to a powerful federal government. A compromise was reached where, in some cases, the federal government has the power, and in other cases, power is reserved for the states. Since that time we have lived with the controversy that this compromise policy has caused.

The sixteenth and seventeenth words of the Constitution are *establish justice*, which are as important as the first three words. A just society gives the game it's ability to survive, but requires by far the most maintenance. Self-interest constantly drives people to cheat and make the game unfair, so it is often necessary to change (repair) the rules to return the game to fairness. Justice is simply fairness, even though many of us limit our definition of justice to the court system. The rest of the words in that first sentence of the Constitution are issues that are related to and reinforce the principle of justice.

Volumes have been written in the attempt to explain the true meanings of the Constitution, often without mentioning those very important first seventeen words. Often lecturers and their books describe the entire Preamble as a meaningless introduction to the real Constitution rather than a statement of founding principles. The definitions of the words used in the preamble during the time that they were written are still the true definitions of those words today. The tragedy is that people with special interests have tried to change those definitions, too often successfully, to satisfy those interests. Fortunately, the fundamentals of a *more perfect* economy were already being put into practice in this country. If we had done a good job of maintaining those economic fundamentals, then our economy and society would still be healthy instead of giving strong indications that it is sick.

3

Capitalism's Basics: Competition; Supply, Demand, and Monopoly; the Evil

CAPITALISM OPERATING WITHOUT equalizing forces always runs amok, creating excess wealth that in turn creates unconstitutional concentration of power away from *We the People*. Adam Smith, the father of modern capitalism, discussed this issue in his 1776 book on political economics, *Wealth of Nations*, in which he stated: "Whenever there is great prosperity, there is great inequality. For one very rich man there must be Five Hundred poor, and the affluence of the few supposes the indignation of the poor who are often driven by want, and prompted by envy, to invade his possessions."

Capitalism's uniform structure is a market where there are entities who produce goods and services, and entities willing and capable of purchasing those goods and services. The equalizing forces necessary on the supply side are availability of product or labor, quality of product or labor, and an attractive price. A healthy demand side requires that money or resources are available to purchasers.

Availability, quality, and price are traditionally controlled by competition. If availability of needed materials or workers is limited, if the quality is poor, or if the price is too high, then other suppliers will seize the opportunity to enter the market and compete in all those areas. A lack of resources, including money on the demand side, will act like competition and correct the supply side excesses, but it will also depress the economy. Thus, supply and demand, corrected by fair competition, are the hallmarks of a healthy capitalist economy. Fair competition controlled by fair rules of the game is the essence of the game of economics. It is an easy statement to make, but a process that is very difficult to carry out.

The competition required for a fair game can be made unfair and ineffective in an almost-unlimited number of ways. The most used ways to reduce competitive power is to make the rules unfair, make new unfair rules, or, better yet, eliminate the rules. These actions tend to create a monopoly that will make it easier to increase price, reduce expenses, or both, making it possible to unfairly increase profits. Making excess profits, due to creating monopolistic power, is one of the objectives of the new free-market system, but it is clear that such excess profits are damaging to both the market and the consumer.

There are many fair ways to compete in the marketplace. A competitor could find a better way to procure raw materials,

innovate better ways of processing raw materials, invent better manufacturing procedures, develop labor-force training
systems to make labor more available, or implement hundreds of other such fair actions.

If a company dominates a market by monopolizing the supply of raw materials or labor, is able to monopolize demand
for product by unfair marketing, or is strong enough to be
able to lower the price below the cost of production, it could
unfairly force a competitor out of the market, damaging both
the market and the consumer. It seems obvious that a greed-
driven market is more likely to use these unfair, competitive
practices to produce greater profit. However, proponents of
this new greed-based free-market philosophy feel that there
is a self-correcting element of human morality in the greed-
based market that will keep it fair. Really?

Those who were born in the early 1900s enjoyed the
game of Monopoly, which came out in 1935. We had great fun
using good luck and inner greed to wipe out our opponents
by monopolizing the hotels on Park Place. Besides being
fun, Monopoly was also educational, teaching us that using
a monopoly as a business practice was a wonderful way to be
very successful, and the best way to create a monopoly was
by using shady, unjust but legal practices. And you can get
away with using shady, unfair practices by making sure there
are few or no fair rules in the game. There was an element
in the Monopoly game that most players didn't realize was
important. Each player was given a certain amount of money
to start the game—without realizing that if the game were
real, they would need to earn the money—thus they needed

to assume that the money was inherited. In the real game of business, the starting money would not be equal, with some players inheriting huge fortunes and with others inheriting none, which means a great inequality of opportunity. It would not be surprising that the one who started with the greatest wealth would win the game.

Chapter 8 discusses propaganda, which is another potent force to block free use of competition in the market. If marketers can gain *mind control* over people who make market decisions by using propaganda, those decisions are more likely to be incorrect and lead to the creation or strengthening of monopolies. This is due to having no rules of the game against propaganda, but developing such rules might be impossible. Intensely educating consumers about propaganda and marketing may be the only possible correcting strategy.

Early in the operation of our country, we tried to keep our economy pure by making sure equality of opportunity was protected by ensuring entrepreneurs could enter the market and compete. It was later found that competition wasn't practical in some types of businesses, so a new type of business called a utility was created. This was especially important in the distribution of electric power. Running multiple power lines through a community would be extremely impractical and would increase costs to the consumer. The options seem to be either having all utilities run by the state or creating a state-controlled private-sector company. Both types of utilities are now common in this country, but private-sector utilities are popular because people feel they are often operated more efficiently. Private-sector utilities are overseen by commissions appointed by the state to make sure that fair practices are followed, costs are practically controlled, and prices and profits are kept reasonable. In other words, a commission takes over the responsibility of competition in managing a utility.

Private utilities, overseen by commission, have worked very well in this country and internationally. As with all market activity, the rules for utilities need to be adjusted occasionally, as some operators will find ways to thwart the rules. The utility systems have been used mainly for utilities that control distribution of such things as electric power, water, and communications. There are many other areas of the market where competition doesn't work well as a controller causing consumers and the economy to be treated unjustly. As a correction to this problem, utility-like companies could be created to better serve the community.

These injustices occur in some parts of the corporate system. Corporations in this country were originally formed to give these businesses certain privileges. To gain these privileges, they were usually expected to follow rules, such as spelling out the purpose of their business in their application, that the product or service would be a benefit to the public, and that profit to the company would be reasonable. In the first few years of the Union corporations were chartered by the states, with each corporation operating and its respective state or states. They could be chartered in several states, but an individual charter was required for each state. Several states chartered corporations for a limited time, some for just one year, and some required that the corporation present evidence that it was operating for their stated purpose and for the benefit of the public. Corporation managers felt that state-by-state chartering was inefficient and a barrier to practical operation, so to remedy this, Congress made it possible for a state to develop a corporation charter that would be good throughout the country, and every state would be required to accept those corporations whether or not they met the requirements of that individual state. The state of Delaware was first to take advantage of the law and developed a corporate law that required corporations to pay their incorporation fee with essentially no other requirements. As a result, many corporations in the United States are incorporated in the state of Delaware to this day. Those corporations have the advantage of avoiding rules, which might be placed on them if they incorporated in their home state. Interestingly, some of those who were most in favor of one state creating a corporation with rules that overrode those of other states were also those who otherwise spoke in favor of increasing states rights over those of the central government.

This caused a change that allowed corporations to be chartered entirely for the benefit of their shareholders and with no requirement to benefit the public. Thus, there are some corporations that have become so monopolistic that they are essentially the only providers of certain products or services, which overall, actually acts as a disservice to the public. These corporations maintain that position by providing acceptable quality and service, while at a price that is high enough to produce excessive profits, but over which the market has no control. Serious examples of this type of corporation are the numerous major healthcare corporations, including healthcare drug-producing corporations. Many maintain their monopolistic power through the patent system. In this case, the market has no control over what products are developed or at what price. Excess price being a restriction of availability to the public would not have been possible. This clout is available because of a patent and because the requirement to produce products for the benefit of the public has been eliminated.

There are cases where the business model has developed to the point that any possibility of control of a general corporation would be impossible, and where competition can have almost no control or would even be practical. There are drugs that are very necessary to the public, which has no choice but to pay the price that is demanded. It seems there is just one answer to this dilemma: the formation of private-sector utility-like corporations. These utility-like corporations would meet all the requirements of a private-sector drug-developing company, except that a commission would replace competition as the controller. Under a utility-like system, drug prices would be a fraction of the current price since the great cost of extreme profits would be gone, as would the high cost of marketing, which could be greater than the cost of drug production. Society would need to assume some of the responsibility for drug creation since need would now be the driver instead of high profit. Drug corporation marketing to the public is not necessary to make proper medicines available, since this should be the prerogative of the professional healthcare provider. Marketing directly to the public actually decreases the efficiency and safety of the system since marketing can lead the patient to request or even demand medications that are less safe or less effective.

People or organizations using their genius to innovate better products and services to benefit society should be rewarded, but should not have the right to steal. Limiting the ability of drug developers to profit from these innovations for a certain time is just, but these rights should not give them the ability to hold the public hostage in providing a product or service that is important for the health and well-being of people. When looked at in the terms of economics, these corporations are more than harmful. They are like other monopolies that can be very destructive to the economy and the well-being of people in need. There should be incentive rewards given to researchers for special acts of discovery, but the rewards should not justify their demands for great wealth.

We have corporations in other industries that, through patterns of mergers, have become essentially monopolies—when competition has been wiped out—to the point that they function more like an electric utility than a normal company that has competition. The Federal Trade Commission had very strong enforceable rules against the development of monopolies and against the elimination of competition, but the rules seem to have been watered down, with unjust activities taking place. The power of those industries in the rule-making bodies of government has become so strong that those injustices would now be very hard to correct. And this power would make it difficult to reconstitute those corporations that have become monopolistic into utility-like corporations. Even so, as in the case of the healthcare industry, it would be a benefit to the public to reconstitute all corporations that have become monopolistic into utility-like corporations. This would mean that a utility-like commission would take the place of the lost competition in protection of the public.

A bedrock principle of the US Constitution establishes that *We the People* are the holders of the power; therefore, concentration of power away from the people through wealth or violence is clearly unconstitutional. But who is responsible for enforcing compliance with this basic principle? This question may be improperly answered through a precedent-setting opinion in the first session of the Supreme Court. John Jay, a Federalist during the Constitutional Convention, was later appointed the first chief justice of the Supreme Court. Chief Justice Jay, in a case before the first court session in 1790, wrote an opinion for the majority in the flowery, wordy language style of the time, which is paraphrased, "those who own this country should run it." His feelings were that "those who own this country" were the landed gentry and other elites, rather than *We the People*. Supreme Court opinions often become precedents that are "cast in stone" rather than reexamined for true constitutionality. The Supreme Court, since that time, often seems to have issued opinions based on that precedent, which has weakened not only the *We the People* principle, but also the major principle of justice. As an example, recently in a decision concerning the Citizens United and the McCutcheon cases deemed unconstitutional rules that control concentration of wealth and power that weakened the power of the people. This was such a blow to those who believe strongly in the principles of the Constitution— of establishing justice and that the people have the power—that it caused several groups to promote a constitutional amendment that would clarify that principle. However, the concentrated power through wealth may be so unbreakable that no change can be made unless citizens find the willingness to force those changes.

4

Our Two Free-Market Economies

MOST AGREE THAT our capitalist system is based on providing a market for the supplier and a choice of goods and services for the consumer. These choices are possible because there are many suppliers of goods, such as manufacturers and importers, and providers of nongovernmental services, such as doctors, repair shops, beauty shops, and barbers. Prices are set by competition between these suppliers and by supply and demand for goods and services. If the supply is adequate and the service is good, but the price is too high, other suppliers are free to enter the market and compete for customers by lowering their price in a system known as the *free* (to enter) *market*. The other important controller of the market is that the economy must make it possible for the consumers to have the money to make purchases in the market. Without that money, the market is no longer free.

A free market is the best system for providing true wellbeing for people. But there are two free markets that have the same name but are almost opposites in their intent;

therefore, when we are talking about the free market, do we mean the *Free Market* or the *free market*? To clarify, we can talk about the two free markets as the *Old Free Market*, which was first described in the mid-eighteenth century, or the *New Free Market*, which appeared in the first half of the twentieth century. Both free markets are still in our conversation today, but it's not clear which free market people are talking about, so naturally there is confusion.

The Old Free Market was first described by Adam Smith in the mid-eighteenth century. At that time, there were very few corporations and only several large corporations. Much of the manufacturing and most of the other businesses were small cottage industries. Usually the customers of these industries either personally knew the manufacturer or at least personally knew the second-in-line distributor. Thus, the relationship between provider and consumer was very personal, with the customer feeling that the provider should put the customer's interests at least equal to or ahead of the provider's self-interests. Providers learned to demonstrate this interest in their customers by providing good quality and services, and also by showing community spirit, that is, showing interest in doing good for the community. If the customers didn't feel that spirit, they were free to seek other providers. Other potential providers would see this lack of community spirit as an opportunity to enter the market and compete. Smith wrote that most potential providers entered the market based solely on self-interest, but soon learned to change their attitudes and, over time, began to appreciate and enjoy the respect shown by consumers who appreciated their good community service. So providers began to do good based on their true desire to do so, rather than the force of the consumer. This was the original meaning of Adam Smith's term the *Invisible Hand*, which leads people to be *moral beings*. The free market then became a wonderful instrument because freedom to enter the market and compete meant that there were few monopolies. Consumers were then free to select the best providers because of competition, which served them well. Freedom to enter the market and compete based on good service and community good actually progressed into many other freedoms, and is the basis of the *Free* in the Old Free Market.

It is fortunate that Adam Smith did his writing in the last half of the 1700s—publishing his great work, *The Wealth Of Nations*, in 1776—so that founders of our Union could learn from it and use the ideas in the development of the Constitution ten years later. Smith used the idea of self-interest to study its effect on the development of societies and their economies. He found that self-interest can be described as a long continuum between the good, which is the need for respect from others, and the bad, which is true greed. Because of what they learned from history and from Smith, our founders tried to design a society that was based on justice (fairness) and—in order to have justice—fair and essential laws.

The New Free Market came about largely from the merging of three related philosophies. The Frankfurt School of Economics emerged as a popular philosophy in the mid-1900s. The leading proponent, Herbert Marcuse, was originally a Marxists in Germany but, after commng to America, changed to believe that greed, even without morality, was the true driver of a good economy. About the same time, Frederick

Hayek brought the philosophy of the Austrian economic system to this country. He taught that extreme self-interest was a legitimate driver of economic activity and that it was a mistake to confuse it with selfishness—a statement that seems beyond rational. He felt strongly that rules (laws) that targeted extreme self-interest were destroyers of healthy economies. He was very influential in leading the then dean of the Chicago School of Economics and Nobel laureate, Dr. Milton Friedman, into writing and teaching about what, at that time, began to be called free market ideas. Later, his student Alan Greenspan became chairman of the Federal Reserve Board of Governors and led the Board to use the New Free Market ideas in many of its decisions.

The third philosophy that strengthened the adoption of New Free Market ideas in the United States was the philosophy of libertarianism. Libertarians taught that there was very little need for central governments and for any laws that interfered with the operation of a capitalist economy. The proponents of the New Free Market like to promote the idea that the free market that was operating from the 1700s to the mid-1900s is the same as the New Free Market, but in actuality they are nearly opposites.

Some of the ideas built into the New Free Market philosophy are good, but the idea of greed for extremely high profit is bad, according to many economists from Smith to the present. There is no evidence that extreme profit benefits the Main Street economy. High profits that generally go up to the macro economy draw money out of the flow of money to the Main Street economy, slowing the economy and harming the average person in our society. Some of the money *dribbles* back, but this amount is much less than the deluge of money going up, never to return. When you question the extreme profiteers about this, they may likely answer, "Yes, but we are the job creators." Supposing that they answer that way, you could say, "If you really believe that, I've got a bridge from Brooklyn to Manhattan that I'm sure you'd like to buy."

A main element of the New Free Market is the privatization of almost everything, but total privatization is the characteristic of concentration of wealth and power. We need to remember that freedom of opportunity and protection from monopoly through fair competition are bedrock principles of our society as well as part of the justice principle of our Constitution. Concentration of wealth and power and undo ownership are dangers to that basic principle of our society. It follows then that excessive privatization is an unjust advantage to those seeking great wealth and power, and against *We the People* having the major power in our country.

Therefore, the New Free Market has become a hindrance and even a danger to our economy and to our society. An example of this danger, now becoming *self evident*, is our healthcare system, which has for over thirty years operated under the New Free Market where greed is the legitimate driver. The core of the system is operated by corporations. Corporations are legally required <u>not</u> to primarily operate for the best interests of its customers, but are required, as their primary responsibility, to meet the economic needs of the stockholders. So if the management of a healthcare corporation needs to decide whether to make a decision that would benefit patients maximally rather than stockholders maximally, they would be putting themselves at legal risk if they decided to maximally benefit the customers (patients). It would be wonderful for the country if we could turn to the newer B Corporation (or Benefit Corporation, or simply B-corps) principle where benefit to the public can legally be the primary objective. B Corporation laws have been established in many states, including Delaware. Non-profit corporations are a separate issue and not general corporations being discussed.

It has become obvious that huge conglomerate business is detrimental to a just economy because of monopolistic practices and the concentration of wealth and power. The changes that have taken place between the time of Adam Smith and the present make it clear that small businesses are the engine that drives a good economy, but that doesn't mean that *large factory* is not considered a small businesses, as long as the company or the same investors don't own the next factory or all the factories in the same business. You can certainly hear wailing and screaming about that statement from the New Free Marketers.

5

The Miracle of the Capitalist Monetary System

THE WONDERFUL CAPITALIST monetary system is a basic building block of all the modern workable societies in the world, but it is also the most complex. The more complex systems become, the more they are subject to manipulation by people who want to concentrate their power. Undo concentration of power, history has taught us, can cause the failure of otherwise great societies.

This means that one of the essential duties of citizens is to protect the systems that have made their society workable and fair. In order to protect these systems, we must first understand them, and understanding very complex systems isn't easy. But if we can find the things that are absolutely fundamental, understanding the political economy becomes easier. Many of these complexities are put in place by those who want to increase their power, and this creates a smokescreen to hide the things that are at the core of the system. These basics were, at one time, well understood by most people, and it is our duty to make sure those basics are understood again.

It is best to start describing the almost-miraculous advantage of a capitalist monetary system and how it all began.

In newer systems of exchange, gold, silver, or a virtual value, such as paper money, are used for exchange rather than the much older system of bringing a pig, wheat, a bicycle, or your offer of labor to fix the storekeeper's roof, in exchange for the shoes or bread that you want in the bartering system.

The newer monetary systems are much more efficient since buyers can take money rather than a pig or wheat to the store to buy a set of dishes for the family or any other item. More importantly, buyers and sellers are now participating in the miracle of <u>flow of money</u>. Let's assume that a storekeeper received payment for the goods he sold in dollars. Those dollars have made him more wealthy, but they have also started a flow of dollars through the economy because he will take his new wealth, the same dollars he received from his customer, to the barber to pay for haircuts for his four young sons. The flow continues because the barber, being now more wealthy, will take those same dollars to a shoe-store owner to purchase new shoes. So far, those same dollars have made three people more wealthy, and besides that, those same dollars will keep flowing from one person to the next, making more and more people wealthy. Even though those dollars are in the hands of each person in the flow for just a short time, each person will get something of value every time they are passed from one person to the next. Thus, each person becomes more wealthy because of dollars previously injected into the flow. This seems simple, but it is a little more complex. The storekeeper can't take all the money he received from the customer to the barber. He must pay for product, pay employees, and pay all other expenses, but all the people who received the expense money will spend the money into the flow, so the effect is the same as if the storekeeper had spent it all in one place. The important thing is that everyone who receives some of the money from the storekeeper spends it into the flow, so the flow is still a single but more complex flow of money; the same dollars keep making more and more people wealthy and the economy grows.

The flow of money economics worked better at the time of the founding of our country because the system was much less complex. The story about the storekeeper, the barber, and the shoe-store owner is an example of this trend. The dollars kept flowing because there was little leakage from the flow of money, even though the money that the storekeeper received was broken into many parts. Leakage is money taken out of the flow, never to return. The money that was paid to them went partly for profit, which they spent maintaining their families and keeping the money in the flow. Some of the money the storekeeper received went to his employees who spent their money in a way that kept it in the flow. Part of the money went to pay for goods that the storekeeper sold. Two hundred years ago, most of the goods he sold came from farmers and small, local *cottage* manufacturers who spent the money they received from the storekeeper on Main Street, where it went back into the flow. Thus, the flow-of-money economic system continued doing its wonders with very little leakage.

Things in a society always become more complex with time. Now, the goods the storekeeper sells come from a great distance, very often from outside the United States. The own-ers of these macro economy industries have great wealth, and they don't need to spend a high percentage of their wealth in the Main Street economy. Most of their income becomes leakage. If the manufacturers are also outside the United States, those employees also spend their money outside the United States, away from Main Street economy, and that money also becomes leakage. These examples of leakage are not illegal or even immoral, but they seriously weaken the flow-of-money system that the middle class depends on for its economic well-being.

Dollars entering the flow and making a series of people wealthy are not the only advantages that society gets from the flow of money. When a number of people get money from the flow, needing haircuts for their family, there is increasing demand on the barber who then needs to hire an assistant barber to meet that demand; thus employment goes up. As this multiplies due to the flow, the increasing demand will require a number of new barbers who will need shoes for their families, so the shoe store will need to increase employment, making the effects of flow of money mushroom. If money doesn't leak out of the flow, then this wonderful effect is self-sustaining. There are a number of ways money can leak out of the flow, and also a number of ways money can come into the flow, such as government money to hire people—for exam-ple, teachers and law enforcement personnel—that adds outside money to the flow. Losing too much money from the flow causes slowdowns, or what we call recessions or depres-sions. If we could just somehow add money to the flow when needed, slowdowns could eventually be controlled naturally without other government action.

The story about the storekeeper, the barber, and the shoe-store owner suggests that the dollars that flow are always the same dollars, but that's not quite true. Those dollars become mingled with other dollars the storekeeper received from his customers, and even though he pays the same number of dollars to the barber, they are probably not the same dollars that he previously received from a customer. He might spend some of those dollars in several different places, but the miracle of flow is still maintained even though they are now part of a more complex flow. As the process continues, those original dollars might become part of hundreds of flows, which may become thousands, and these flows fuse together into one giant flow. In a well-ordered society, this huge flow becomes stronger and faster over time. This is the real cause of economic growth in a truly capitalist economy, as was outlined many years ago by Adam Smith.

The miracle of flow of money could continue almost indefinitely, except that for many reasons, money tends to leak out of the flow, which causes leakage. In a well-functioning economy, new money coming into the flow tends to balance money that leaks out, and the economy remains strong. This flow of money is the miracle of an economy with a monetary system or, under some definitions, the true capitalist system.

A person doesn't need a PhD in economics to understand how this miracle works. It's very simple. Go down to Main Street and watch it happen. As you watch and study this flow, it becomes obvious that a healthy flow requires two things: one, there needs to be a stream of money constantly entering the flow; and two, the flow needs to be controlled to minimize leakage. If either of these two requirements are lacking, the flow begins to slow, called a recession, or stops, called a depression. Having such a wonderful flow of money is probably too good to be true because of complexities that have been added to the system, but it could happen if leakage was controlled and the economy game was played fairly.

Many officials in our society feel that the slowing of the flow in a recession is caused by too much government debt, so they want to reduce debt by laying off public employees—such as teachers, policeman, and firemen—or by other austerity tactics, which as you can now see will actually decrease the flow as well as intensify the recession, because employment is the well that puts money into the flow. Think back to the shoemaker and his employees who put money into that flow. This was well demonstrated in 2008–2009 when austerity tactics increased the intensity of a recession, changing it into a super recession. Therefore, a more reasonable action would be to increase public employment rather than to decrease it.

Critics say, "That all sounds good, but where does the money come from to pay the teachers, policeman, and firemen without increasing debt?" Debt or some other financing strategy would be necessary to meet those expenses, but as the flow increases as a result of spending that money, tax income will increase and the debt can be repaid if proper fiscal policy is maintained. Other strategies to finance those employment expenses will be discussed in a later chapter.

A dollar put into a flow-of-money system is used again and again, causing the value of the dollar in the economy to be multiplied by the number of times it changes hands before it is lost from the flow. This is the miracle of the flow-of-money system. The economic literature calls the miracle of flow of money the *multiplier effect*. If a dollar stays in the flow for ten exchanges without leakage, its value to the economy becomes ten dollars.

Another part of the miracle of the flow of money is described in modern economic literature as the *velocity of money*, whereby the faster money flows, more people become wealthy, and the economy grows faster. The discussion of money flow in current literature becomes very complex and hard to understand. A truly simple system has been redesigned into something complex and sometimes unworkable, when one or both of the requirements of a good flow-of-money system is lost and the economy stumbles.

The English economist of the early twentieth century, John Maynard Keynes, is considered by some to be the father of the flow-of-money system. He didn't talk a lot in the literature about the flow of money itself, but about the importance of the *demand side* of an economy, which is really in some ways the same thing. He taught that in order to have a good economy, people had to have money to purchase goods and services, which causes the flow of money through the economy. He also understood that if people were to have money, it had to first get into the flow, that is, start the flow. As money flowed through the economy, people would have wealth in the form of spendable money, which would create *demand* for goods and services. Demand would come first, but it would be answered by increases in the *supply* of goods and services because unmet demand creates oportunity for people to enter the market and compete for those dollars that demand has provided. Thus, the critical point in economics is that increase in demand precedes supply, not the other way around. After demand creates supply, this supply of goods and services would be created by people working and earning money by producing goods and services. This money would be pumped into the flow, increasing the miracle of flow of money, but after demand has forced an increase in supply. Timing is also important. The rate that demand increases can't be greater than the ability of supply to increase, because if demand increases faster than supply, prices will rise and inflation will result. The shortage of supply of goods and services would cause the price of goods and services to increase. When stimulating increases in demand during the recovery from a downturn, the demand needs to be controlled to avoid excessive inflation. This adjustment in the rate of demand is not automatic and must be controlled by a source other than a special interest. This source is the state, which is constitutionally the people. The people exercise their power through their government. The system of economic adjustment is "near perfect" as long as government has not been co-opted through concentration of power by special interests.

The near halt in the flow of money following the 1929 crash produced the Great Depression. Most jobs for the average American were lost, and money generated by employment stopped. This, of course, almost stopped the stream of money into the flow, halting the basic requirement for a

flow-of-money system. Unfortunately, the country was operating under an opposite type of economy called the *supply
side* economy. The belief of those who teach *supply side* economics is that supply precedes demand. Under this economy,
it was believed the only thing that was needed to stimulate an
economy was to produce more goods and services to be purchased, thus increasing the flow of money. Manufacturers and
others were encouraged by the government to increase supply
of goods and services. There is an obvious problem. It does little good to increase supply if there is little demand, and there
is little demand if people have little money. Management
of larger businesses realized that increasing supply without
demand would be unwise; therefore, nothing happened and
the economy continued the disastrous Depression. It's interesting that the *Henry Ford Rule* was popular about fifteen
years before the Depression. Henry Ford believed that he
needed to pay his workers higher wages because they needed
the money to increase demand for his cars, which is possibly
where FDR got his ideas for economic recovery.

The Depression had started because gambling in the
market had overvalued banks and major businesses. The
more-savvy investors in the stock market knew this, but they
planned to ride the boom as long as possible before the inevitable downturn, at which time they began selling their stocks
before the crash happened. The day the most-savvy investors
decided it was time to sell, other investors were watching for
a sell signal, and everybody began to sell. This caused the
crash that wiped out many businesses, eventually including
the major banks, which in turn wiped out a high percentage of
employment, and thus money from the flow.

The Depression had been underway for some time when President Franklin Roosevelt took office. Roosevelt was a follower of many of Dr. Keynes teachings and immediately began to lead Congress to make changes in government spending, to start the flow of money. He knew this was necessary because the private sector was in no condition to add money to the flow. Roosevelt did this by channeling direct payments to all those unemployed, called *Relief.* This was cash given directly by the government. This money began to immediately start the flow that increased demand, slowly stimulating the increase in supply. Increasing supply required companies to slowly increase employment, which further increased flow of money that began to decrease the agony of extreme poverty. But more was needed. The president developed a system of make-work jobs, the WPA, or Works Progress Administration. The WPA wasn't very efficient in getting work done, but it did do a good job of distributing more money to the people so they could further speed the flow of money and the recovery. The Civilian Conservation Corps, or CCCs, for young men was a wonderful program that resulted in thousands of infrastructure-improvement projects and conservation programs. Most of their pay was sent home to assist their poverty-stricken families. Many of the things that were built are still in use today. The government also started planning a number of huge construction projects around the country to give more people real work with real wages. It was very fortunate that two of the projects, Grand Coulee Dam and Boulder Dam (later called Hoover Dam) in the West were quickly started. These dams were completed just as the Second World War started. Without the huge amount of electric power these dams were immediately able to produce, the efforts of the aluminum industry and the warplane manufacturing industry in the West would have been more difficult, and the war could have been lost without these industries.

We were on the gold standard at that time, which meant that all of our currency had to be backed by an equal amount of gold stored at Fort Knox. Thus, all the money needed for pump priming had to be borrowed in the private macro economy, and even that economy was short of money. Some wealthy foreign investors still had money, and they came to the rescue by making loans to the Treasury. As we went off the gold standard late in the Depression, we then had the ability to *print* money based on the credit or *promise* of the people; we now have much more flexibility to begin pump priming in the event of a downturn. If that ability to print money had been available in 1929 through 1935, recovery from the Great Depression could have been much quicker, but only if the money had been dumped into the Main Street economy to stimulate the flow of money.

The economy of the United States went into deep recession in the years around 2008. Many of our leaders felt that the recession was caused by having too much federal debt, causing our government to deal with this by drastically reducing spending for things in this country. Employment in all parts of the federal government was reduced. This led to reductions in state employment, county employment, city employment, and essentially all employment. Thus, the stream of money entering the flow began to seriously slow.

The Federal Reserve Bank has to keep, as one of its responsibilities, the economy stable. The bank took action with the approval of Congress that involved "priming the pump" as Roosevelt did, which was correct based on what we know about stimulating the miracle of the flow of money. This created lots of money, assumed to be several trillion dollars. The money was created by printing it to a computer record system, and the Federal Reserve Bank immediately anointed the money with a value based on the faith and credit of the people of the United States. In other words, all of us took on the debt of backing that money. However, there is little risk since there is no mechanism for collecting the money from the people. The ability to print money is actually a benefit to the people because it makes it possible to "prime the pump" when there would otherwise be no available money. The disaster was that on the way to the pump, they spilled much of the money.

The money was, of course, only symbolically spilled. Traditionally, the Federal Reserve loans the money it has created to banks, especially the large banks, at a low interest rate of one-quarter to one-half percent. The plan is that the banks will then have money to loan to companies so they can began hiring people to expand the supply of goods (supply-side thinking), increasing consumption and thus stimulating the economy. It would be fruitless for companies to increase supply of goods when there was little money flowing into the Main Street economy to purchase these additional goods. The companies would profit better by using the money to do such things as purchase other companies to increase efficiency and

reduce competition. The cheap money was also used to purchase government bonds yielding a higher interest rate than
the Fed charged. If the government bonds had been used
for public works projects or for increasing public employment, much of the money would then have gone directly
into the Main Street economy. Instead, the new money was
used for such things as paying for the wars and other foreign
expenses—while public employment was being cut, throw-
ing thousands out of work and stopping the flow of money
those people would have produced. It is true that some of the
money used for wars and war materials would *dribble* back
down to the Main Street economy, but much more of that
money would have arrived on Main Street if it'd been directly
sent through public works projects, thereby increasing public
employment.

The thinking that caused most of the stimulus problems
arose with Dr. Keynes not recognizing the fact that there are
two economies—and that fact bears repeating.

The macro economy is worldwide and operates somewhere above those of us down on terra firma, and it is owned
by the large banks, especially international banks; the large
corporations, especially international corporations; wealthy
individuals internationally; and in some cases, the governments of the world. The macro economy is controlled by those
who "own" it, and public policy has little effect since those
same owners have control over most regulation. People in US
communities operate in the Main Street economy, which we
know and understand. The two economies are very different,
and when an attempt is made to control the macro economy,

it can have little positive effect on the Main Street economy; and since the macro economy takes money from the Main Street economy, the effect on the majority of the public is always negative.

At the time of the Great Depression, Dr. Keynes coined the term *liquidity trap*, which meant that pushing money into the economy for stimulation often failed because households saved the money rather than spending it, which did not increase the flow of money. Thus the money, he believed, got trapped in households. This was false thinking because the money pushed into the economy got trapped in the macro economy and never made it to households. The idea that households would receive stimulus money and instead save it was hard to imagine, as households had no money until under the New Deal, when the Roosevelt administration began sending money directly to the people, who immediately spent it. It is preposterous to think that people who are hungry would save money rather than spend it to buy food, clothing, or other essentials.

The liquidity-trap thinking surfaced again at the start of the great recession in 2008. The stimulus money was directed to the banks rather than directly to the people on Main Street, partly because of the fear that the people would save the money rather than spend it. Some people in the elite community never seem to understand the panicked feelings of people whose families are facing extreme poverty. If Dr. Keynes and the other major economists had realized that there were two economies, they would not have made those mistakes. We know that a little money can dribble down to the Main

Street economy from the macro economy, but not enough to be effective in a recession, and that greater amounts of money can flow up from the Main Street economy to the macro economy, causing blockage to a recovery in a downturn.

Dr. Keynes made one suggestion in 1933 that would have helped the flow of money on Main Street. He suggested the government should bury money in glass jars all over the country so that people could dig them up to retrieve the money and spend it. Unfortunately, he was just joking, but the idea of directly distributing money to help people to stimulate the economy during a downturn has become mainstream. We now have such things as food stamps and unemployment payments to serve those exact purposes. Unfortunately, the amount of stimulus money funneled into the Main Street economy has been seriously insufficient and has done only minimal good.

Economic downturns increase the problem because money going into the flow decreases along with income to the Treasury, and additional sources of money are necessary to pay for any increased public employment or public works projects. The only mechanism we have had for financing these needs has been public debt. People are horrified at the thought of public debt, but when it is used to restart the flow of money in a recession or depression, the benefits of debt far outweigh the disadvantages. This debt fear seems to be based on a Thomas Tusser statement often quoted by Benjamin Franklin, "Who goeth a borrowing / Goeth a sorrowing." Franklin often preached against going into debt, so it has become a cornerstone of American thinking. This has been good advice for American families, but limits the use of a good tool in government policy; however, debt is always bad if the money is wasted.

It is important that stimulus money pumped into the Main Street economy is carefully controlled so it doesn't outdo the supply of goods and services, causing inflation. Sometimes the supply of goods in a downturn also needs to be stimulated to promote rapid recovery without inflation.

There are two ways this stimulus spending could be financed, but because of unjust rules, the country is limited to just one at the moment. The present system allows the Federal Reserve to print the money that is then given value by the faith and credit of the people, and then loaned at a very low interest rate to the banks. The US Treasury would pay the bills by issuing Treasury bonds and selling them to the banks. The banks, using the money they borrowed at a low rate from the Federal Reserve, would purchase the bonds from the Treasury and receive a higher interest rate than they pay the Federal Reserve for the newly created money. The Federal Reserve calls this method of stimulating the economy, through creating money and loaning it to the big banks, *quantitative easing*. Some feel it should be called stimulating the economy through stimulating bank profits.

If laws would allow it, the Federal Reserve could create the money, have it guaranteed by the faith and credit of the people, and give the money directly to the US Treasury. The US Treasury could then directly pay the public works projects bills and other bills when the income to the Treasury is otherwise insufficient. There would be no interest charge or set repayment plan; therefore, this would *not* become national debt.

The deal for the public would be much better with the direct-payment system, except that there are rules and laws against direct payment of government bills. Somehow the rules have been set so that the only way bills can be paid is by the creation of national debt. This type of program would need to be carefully regulated, preventing the possibility of runaway inflation. If the amount of money directly given to the Treasury was the same amount that would be given through the issuance of bonds, then the effects on the economy would be equal and would not increase the debt problem. There would be no inflation risk from that money if the rate of flow into the economy was regulated to be balanced by increases in supply. Therefore, stimulus money going into the flow of money through employment in a downturn should be carefully regulated, whether it is from the issuing of bonds or the printing of money.

Under the present system, regulation of the economy is the duty of the Federal Reserve, but the Federal Reserve is essentially controlled by the big banks, and the banks would logically have little interest in creating a new system that would be a change from the bond system that is so lucrative. Debt is sometimes a good public policy tool, but debt must be repaid through tax policy where interest is included, which is a drag on the Treasury.

If the newly created money had been directly given to federal agencies for public works employment or to other private- and public-sector employment—with jobs such as teachers, firemen, law enforcement personnel, healthcare workers, and others—no additional bonds would be needed, and the federal debt would not be increased. All the additional people who are employed would begin paying taxes, and these extra taxes would eventually pay back the pump-priming money. Money printed by the Federal Reserve does not have to be repaid if it isn't turned into debt-creating bonds, but should be repaid if there is a chance of creating inflation by an over-supply of money.

If it was made legally possible, there could be other advantages to increasing money supply by printing money. We have been paying for a trade deficit by borrowing money in the United States or from foreign investors who purchase US Treasury bonds. This creates national debt. If we created (printed) the money to pay the trade deficit, it would not become debt. Unnecessary debt is bad for the economy since it creates an interest load on the taxpayers. Creating money would increase the supply of dollars, which because of dilution, would tend to decrease the dollars' value, and in some cases this would be good. Our trading partners have, in some cases, manipulated the value of their currency, making their currency cheaper when compared to the dollar. This makes American goods more expensive in the international marketplace, giving an unfair competitive advantage to some foreign producers, which decreases the US export market. A less-valued dollar would make American goods less costly and easier for people in other markets to buy, thus increasing our exports. This would increase employment and production in the United States with the much-needed effect of decreasing poverty.

This type of change in our monetary strategy would cause some probable losses for the macro economy, but it would reduce concentration of wealth in that economy. Wealth equals power, and concentration of power is always a bad thing.

This probably wouldn't completely stop the almost-exclusive use of Chinese consumer products in the United States. Even if these products cost more, it is improbable that China's competitive advantage in consumer products can be changed, but we can develop other products in areas such as energy, transportation, the environment, and infrastructure to compensate or develop a much larger service economy to better serve the people of this country and increase the export of services.

6

The Miracle is Lost in the Great Burglary: Part 1

THE GREAT BURGLARY took place in the 1970s and 1980s when someone stole most of the rules of the game. Some of the stolen rules involved our society generally, but the greatest effect took place when the rules of the game of economics disappeared. To understand this, another look at the system is necessary.

Most developed countries have two separate economic systems, the macro economy and the Main Street economy. The system that most of us work in is the Main Street economy. This is a system where the flow of money is the main ingredient, and it is where at least 80 percent of us live. This is where we earn and spend our money on not only Main Street but also the entire country. For those of us in the 80 percent, it is our economy, and since it is a game, we have tried to keep the rules fair. For a long time, *We the People* were able to make workable the rules for our economy, but starting in the 1970s, somebody else began making the rules or the rules disappeared altogether—the Great Burglary.

The Main Street economy is a system that, if operated properly, will function in an efficient way, bringing wealth and well-being to the people automatically; but as we can see, this great benefit doesn't always happen. The reason for this can be better understood if we look at the Main Street economy as a game, a very serious game, much like the game of Monopoly or even the game of football. These last two games work quite well and seldom fall into chaos, but our Main Street economy game often does; so it's important to look for the reasons why these first two games work well, but our big Main Street economy game often doesn't. When we look closely, we see that the reason our regular games work properly is that they have rules of fair play. If football had no enforced fair rules, it would soon fall into confusion and chaos. Even if most of the players tried to play the game following the tradition of good sportsmanship, some would not, thus making the game unplayable. It's interesting that football is more like the economy game than most other games. The game is highly competitive and has a rough-and-tumble way about it, which is still within the rules of fairness. It works well. The Main Street economy is, like our society generally, based on the rule of law. The rule of law is essentially the rule of fairness, just like the rules of football, and if the rules of the Main Street economy were fair just like the rules of football, that game would also work well. If the rules of football were weakened or eliminated, then the game of football would also fail, similar to when our economy fails when just rules are lacking. One professor of economics quips that for years, those with special interests have worked to weaken the rules of the economy game, but in the last thirty years, they found it's best to just eliminate the rules altogether, usually by calling them confusing, unneeded red tape.

There are a number of Main Street economies around the world; however, the macro economy has become global and international and is in many ways a single economy. The power of the macro economy can be thought of as functioning somewhere up above, in the ether, and it is somewhat a mystery to those of us on earth, even though we live every day with the tools that are used. The tools are the major banks worldwide, huge multinational corporations, large corporations within the country, other large private-sector businesses, and many units of government that the macro economy controls. Most, not all, of these on the list operate under the philosophy of the greed-driven New Free Market where profit is primary and public good is secondary.

Preventing undue leakage is the purpose of many of the rules governing our flow of money in the Main Street economy. The rules of that economy are intended to be made by representatives of the people, under the principle of *establishing justice* set forth in our Constitution. However, the macro economy profits from the Main Street economy, so *they*, the owners of the macro economy, are careful to see that no rules are made prohibiting leaking money from the flow up to the monster macro economy. Some of this money dribbles down the flow, but it is usually a dribble as compared to the gusher going up. The reason that so little of this money returns to the flow is that when it arrives up in the macro economy, it goes to huge banks and multinational corporations that keep it for their own purposes, or they send it out of the country where most of the money is lost to the international macro economy. Therefore, our workers gain little money, thus little money can be added to the Main Street flow of money—a serious cause of leakage. The owners of the macro economy use many arguments to attempt to convince those in the Main Street economy that this flow of money up to the macro economy is a great benefit to those on Main Street. Unfortunately, the benefit goes almost entirely to those at the top.

Taxes that are avoided could be used to provide services and infrastructure for the Main Street economy and society. Instead, they become leakage in the system. There are many strategies for this tax avoidance that are legal but not moral. A major strategy for tax avoidance is used when companies move headquarters and manufacturing out of the country, which makes it possible for them, in many cases, to avoid paying US taxes. One large US company that moved only its headquarters out of the country calculated that it will save one hundred million dollars in taxes each year, and its shareholders should save more! Over one hundred major companies have moved headquarters out of the country since 1983. Think of what those billions of dollars could have accomplished had they been collected and moved into the Main Street flow-of-money economy.

Spokesmen for the managers of the macro economy claim emphatically that leakage up to the macro economy is not a problem, even though it is so apparent it could be considered self-evident. *They* claim the leakage problem is due to taxation. It is true that taxation is part of the problem, though it shouldn't be. If taxation were used for the direct benefit of the people, such as employing teachers, police, firefighters, infrastructure maintenance people, and the myriad of other government-sponsored public service employees, these employees would spend their money on Main Street, and thus immediately return it to the flow. It would not be leakage. But if we spend the tax money in a way that bypasses the Main Street economy, nothing goes back to the flow, so leakage takes place.

Taxation is one area where people with special interests can have great influence over making the rules. Our administrators and Congress need to be vigilant about correcting the rules when these injustices take place. Increasing evidence shows that many of those administrators and legislators responsible for keeping the rules fair are unduly influenced by owners of the macro economy, and they fail in their responsibility to the public. Besides causing economic imbalances, this influence causes concentration of power and thus imbalances in our entire society.

The leakage most cherished by those who own the macro economy is the great amount of money going to the macro economy from excess profit. Excess profit is profit from a business operation gained by monopolistic activity, unfair practices, or excess income taken from a business by owners or management. In each case, this profit is beyond what will reasonably be used to pay expenses into the Main

Street economy, so it goes to the macro economy, never to return.

Our political economics guru, Adam Smith, in 1776 also had wisdom for us on this subject: "Our merchants and Masters complain of the bad effects of high wages in raising the price and lessening the sale of goods. They say nothing concerning the bad effects of high profits. They are silent with regard to the pernicious effects of their own gains. They complain only of those of other people."

What about savings? It depends on what the savings are for. If the savings are to be used to pay later Main Street expenses or for retirement, that money remains in the flow, but it's a delayed flow. Savings have little effect on the flow for two reasons. Money coming out of savings to be spent and money going into savings should eventually balance out, so the Main Street flow of money is not affected. Secondly, banks can be of great service to the Main Street economy by using deposited savings to loan to those in need of financing who will spend it, causing the money to immediately return to the flow. Besides having reduced flow, the danger from all that money laying up in the macro economy is that if the owners or managers of the macro economy should decide to bring a large amount of that money down, quickly injecting it into the Main Street economy, that money would cause a sudden surge of demand and serious inflation, which could destroy the Main Street economy. It's like a black cloud hanging over all of us. The people need to began considering some sort of a wealth-reduction program to bring that black cloud under control—possibly a high estate tax without loopholes. This may be a problem since we would feel terrible about the plague of cardiac arrests that would take place among the owners of the macro economy if there was even a thought of such a thing.

6

The Miracle is Lost in the Great Burglary: Part 2

THE MIRACLE OF the capitalist monetary system oper-ating in a Main Street–type flow-of-money economy is real and wonderful, but the greed-based macro economy has been in a life-and-death battle with the Main Street economy for two hundred or more years. This battle is characterized by the macro economy trying to eliminate the Main Street economy and the Main Street economy struggling to main-tain itself as the People's economy. The score in this battle or game is about to come up on the scoreboard, and it is, the greed-based macro economy, one– the miracle Main Street economy, zero.

In 1760, the Rothschild family founded the first truly inter-national macro economy. Mayer Amschel Rothschild and his five sons in Germany founded a company as an international banking company. The five Rothschild sons were sent to the five recognized financial capitals of the world to set up banks. By the turn of the century, the Rothschild family, using this macro economic strategy, was involved in most of the major businesses around the world and were also considered by far to be the richest family in history. The company has always been secretive about its operations, and much mythology has developed; however, several things are known for sure. A well-documented story was that one Rothschild son was sent to London to manage the financial operation in England. The son named Mayer arranged for a mercenary army to aid British forces in overwhelming Napoleon at Waterloo. Rothschild rushed back to England with advanced knowledge of that conflict, allowing him to leak information that England had lost the war. This caused bond prices to crash. He then bought all the bonds available in England, and then released the true information that England had won the war, causing bond prices to soar. After this, he began to sell the bonds, making the largest profit in history up to that time. The Rothschilds apparently owned the acro economy until sometime in the 1800s, when others became powerful enough to become included. The philosophy that was established for the macro economy was that anything, no matter how immoral, was encouraged if it led to making high profits. A famous quote is attributed to the founding Rothschild, "Give me control of a nation's money and I care not who makes the laws." This quote, as thought by some, has become the motto of the international banking community and, in recent history, the entire macro economy.

At least 80 percent of US families depend on the person-to-person flow of money for their livelihood and well-being. If money leaks out of the flow with little flowing in, then over time, the miracle of Main Street economy is going to stall. Oh well, we think, too bad—fortunately, the wonderful, other economy up there somewhere will take care of us. The

1 percent that runs the ethereal macro economy, along with the possible 19 percent who are *fellow travelers*, have the best interests of the 80 percent at heart and will support our survival with feelings of well-being so we can continue our "pursuit of happiness." Really?

What's happened to the miracle economy that at one time worked so well? To understand that, look at one transaction on Main Street that should be part of the flow of money. A storekeeper sells a shovel to a farmer in the community and takes in dollars. To make the flow-of-money miracle work, those dollars need to be returned to the flow. So here's what happened in the past. The storekeepers sent most of the dollars to the manufacturer for the shovel. The manufacturer, who is usually someone nearby, pays the handle maker, who will spend his money in the flow. Some of the manufacturer's money will go to his employees in the machine shop, who spend it back into the flow. Some money will go for taxes, which should be used to pay government employees, such as office workers at City Hall, and many others who will spend their wages back into the flow. So the money from the shovel sale positively affects many people by returning the money to the flow after each exchange.

But if the storekeeper had purchased the shovel from a manufacturer in China, most of the dollars would go to China via a multinational importer. How much of that money would return to the flow? You are right—zilch! Also, when the storekeeper buys the shovel from a local manufacturer, the manufacturer, his employees, and many others down the line pay taxes on their incomes, as generated by selling the shovel, which makes the local, state, and federal tax incomes higher. If multiplied by millions of such sales, the tax incomes make it possible for the government to be able to pay for needed public services without creating debt. In this country, as in most countries, taxes are generated from the production of goods and services, especially from the payroll taxes on labor. So in the case of the shovel, the foreign importer—which is quite likely a multinational corporation based in this country—has, in effect, stolen those taxes. Also, our storekeeper has to pay higher taxes (along with the rest of us) because the needed taxes were stolen, rather than going into the flow where the taxes would have been multiplied several times as the shovel money became taxable income for a number of people down the line.

Think of the shovel scenario playing out billions of times every day where the flow of dollars for much of the production of goods and services is stolen by bypassing the Main Street flow. The important loss is the money that would have been paid as wages to employees of all those businesses down the line if the shovel production hadn't been outsourced.

The thing that causes this problem, as you can see, is what is called globalization, but that's a confusing term. The business-school term is outsourcing, and it is based on the rule that states, "grow revenues, while shrinking costs, and increase profits or stated clearly—_outsourcing._" Outsourcing means sending all work somewhere where it can be done much less expensively, meaning another country where labor and other costs are much lower. This would not be a problem if an amount of goods equal to the imports were exported from the United States, equalizing the effect of labor costs, but this hasn't happened for many years.

Much of the public misunderstanding of this problem is caused by the misuse of terms. Trade with other countries is good, and it is responsible for much of the economic growth in this country. Trade means just what it says, one country trades its goods for goods of another country. It is an equal or nearly equal two-way activity. Trade can become more complex, but still fair, when one country trades its goods to a second country, which then trades its goods to a third country, and the third country trades its goods back to the first country so that in the end, each country gives and receives equal value. Outsourcing is importing goods or services from another country without any requirement for an exchange of goods or services back to that country or another country. So outsourcing means just what it says. A company has goods produced in other countries, to be sold back in this country at a low price to weaken competition and make higher profits. The bad, nearly criminal thing is that this <u>outsourcing</u> is called *trade* by those wanting to confuse the public into supporting this travesty. This outsourcing is sometimes called *globalization* to even further confuse the public.

Globalization is the term used instead of *outsourcing* in order to gloss over the fact that outsourcing is a macro economy business tactic. Our retailers seldom buy goods directly from a foreign manufacturer. They buy goods from an American manufacturer who has outsourced the actual production to a place where labor costs, along with costs for environmental and safety regulation, are many times lower, and they can pay for labor and expenses with local currency that is much less valuable than U.S. currency.

The illustration about the storekeeper and the shovel demonstrates how slowing the flow of money on Main Street increases profits for the macro economy while decreasing income for the Main Street economy, which validates the out-sourcing business rule when profit and monopoly are the only considerations.

While talking about outsourcing as reducing the value of labor worldwide, it is interesting that Karl Marx, who wrote the handbook on communism in the 1800s, also wrote a book on economics, *Das Kapital*, a critique on unfair capitalism in that excess profit is made from reducing the value of labor. Marx lived at a time when the macro economy was becoming dominant. This is where Karl Marx possibly got his ideas. He felt that capitalism could become just and fair by increasing the value of labor to where there was balance. He believed that capital and labor, working as a team, could produce a better society than when they were in combat. Marx made a terrible mistake when he invented communism, but he may have been at least partially correct when he talked about capital and labor, since that is the core of the outsourcing dilemma.

Marx was late with his ideas. Adam Smith, stated 150 years earlier in his work *Wealth of Nations*, "labor, therefore, it appears evidently, is the only universal, as well as the only accurate, measure of value, or the only standard by which we can compare the value of different commodities, at all times, and all places." He reasoned that the best evidence for this was made clear at the time of division of labor, eons before.

7

Opportunity: The Hallmark Right in Our Society and Economy

Individual Initiative: The Requirement for Seizing Opportunity

OUR LEADERS DURING the establishment of our new country dreamed of creating a *more perfect* society. Since before the Romans and the Greeks, leaders have tried to develop such a society, and they sometimes seemed to be on the road to success, only to have the society fail. The societies of Europe in the eighteenth century, the ones that the founders of our union were using as a pattern, had great faults. Most of the power was concentrated at the top, with many societies having kings or emperors that maintained all the power, although some European societies had systems of justice that gave some guarantees of fairness and liberty to their subjects.

Our founders hoped to establish a society that could avoid the problems that had plagued earlier societies. Several framers of the Constitution were scholars who had studied the Roman Republic and the short-lived Greek democracy for clues as to what caused their breakdown. They found that the causes were so complex that it was hard to find a single cause, but they did find that in both cases, it was clear that <u>concentration of power away from the people was the most important cause.</u> The Romans set up a representative government where both the representatives and leaders were in power for a very short time, and during that time, the leaders and representatives were expected to work only for the best interests of the people. The Greek system, which comprised mostly the city of Athens, was governed primarily through great meetings of the people, and they somehow came to decisions in these meetings. It was apparently felt that people who met together would be better able to prevent power from concentrating. It was also clear that if all the people had an opportunity to participate, both majorities and minorities would be treated justly, which is the characteristic of a democracy. In a republic, the majority rules, and minorities are sometimes treated less fairly.

Our leaders decided to use what was learned from these two early societies and others to make a number of improvements and to consider these improvements as experimental. These improvements would be carefully monitored so that corrections could be made before unforeseen problems caused damage. This plan was even known at the time as the great experiment.

The guiding principle that Madison, Hamilton, and others fought for during the Constitutional Convention was that all power would be vested in the people, and structures would be put in place to make sure that the power was never taken from the people by a concentration of power. This would eliminate the great fault in the earlier societies. Of equal importance was the establishment of a system of justice and, more importantly, that a system would be put in place to make sure that it remained just. This was to be done by establishing a Supreme Court made up of scholars in the science of justice who are special people, carefully chosen to be without bias. This requirement of qualifications for membership, was an understanding, but not actually written into the Constitution. This is unfortunate since neither the President nor the Senate have been required to be sure these attributes were in place before appointing a member to the court.

The discussions leading up to the writing and adoption of the Constitution involved defining the principles that were identified, and then establishing a structure to implement those principles. Although principles were understood, they were not actually written as the preamble until later in the project. It was understood from the preliminary discussions that the principal to establish justice was not only to establish courts and judges but also to establish the meaning of justice, which would be done by law over time. The thinking of philosophers and economists of the time was that opportunity should not be unfairly or unjustly blocked in a democratic society, and the policy of the framers followed that advice but left it generally under the principle statement—establish justice. That was unfortunate since there were those who believed the only important objective, rather than establishing justice, was meeting the needs of those who, in John Jay's words, "own the country."

Adam Smith taught that a just society and a just economic system needed to be constructed simultaneously almost as one system, and that the system needed to be based on rewarding self-interest without greed as the driver of an economy based on equality of opportunity. He believed that if a person had the opportunity to educate himself (not much gender equality at the time), worked diligently, and had the opportunity to enter the market, then he would very likely become more wealthy. This would not be considered an inequality since the equality was in the opportunity and not the outcome. This is the difference, according to Smith, between a just capitalist system and the social welfare system being proposed by some European planners. In other words, people should be given opportunity rather than welfare, although Smith felt that welfare in a society was essential for those people who have met with serious misfortune.

Another principle of conservative thinking that was prevalent at that time and even more prevalent today is that opportunity by itself is not enough. Individual initiative is the other requirement that makes the system work. Without individual initiative, there is no one to seize opportunity, and economic progress does not happen. In socialist or social welfare systems, individual initiative is dampened and becomes the main barrier to success in those systems. So what is the problem with our market system? In market capitalism, individual initiative is stimulated through a reward system based on the potential creation of great wealth. This means that individual initiative, which is principally driven by accumulation of wealth, is also driven by greed. Great wealth usually leads to concentration of power through wealth. Therefore, the power of *We the People* is diminished along with equality of opportunity. Therein lies the problem, but is there any alternative answer to that problem? Adam Smith taught that if people who were seizing opportunities through operating businesses were forced by public pressure to operate the businesses primarily for the good of the public, the market system would work without creating undue power and without reducing power of the people. He observed that entrepreneurs who serve the good of the community received the goodwill of the people, and after a time, so appreciated that goodwill that they served the good of the community without pressure. Unfortunately, business activity has become so complex that there is a disconnect between the business and the public, as far as pressure is concerned. It will probably need rules requiring businesses to operate in a competitive environment primarily for the good of the public. Businesses that have concentrated great power do not like rules. Therefore, it is up to an informed and concerned public to find the power to make the corrections.

Is individual initiative unduly constrained in our society? If the requirement for power to seize opportunity is mostly inherited rather than acquired through individual initiative, is that congruent with a just society? Is there any way to correct that in a society that has great concentrations of wealth and power? Even if they had the power, the question is how does the public establish a system of equal opportunity? To do so, they would need to limit the freedom that some people are given or have taken for themselves because that freedom could impinge on the freedom of others, especially the freedom of opportunity. For example, what if monopolies became dominant, leaving very little opportunity to enter the market? What if our policy of the absolute right to own private property became so embedded that little property is available for others, limiting the opportunity of private-property ownership? What if guilds became so powerful that there was no opportunity to enter a service profession without being a member of a certain family? There are hundreds of other limitations to opportunity that can take place. To eliminate these barriers to opportunity would require violating some of the rights that have been granted to some of the people. This problem was too complex for drafters of the Constitution to deal with at that time, so it was left to Congress and the Supreme Court to establish justice in that area of the political economy at some future time. Is it possible that time has yet to come?

There were many at the Constitutional Convention who felt strongly that certain rights needed to be made absolute, such as the right to hold slaves, even if those rights were found to unjustly diminish the freedom of others. This led to, among other things, the Bill of Rights, which was added after the main Constitution was completed. As a result, we have a Constitution that prohibits challenging any of those listed rights, and some have become a problem. The assumed right to equality of opportunity, a self-evident right under the *establish justice* principle in the preamble, has never been challenged, but to some extent slowly drifted away. This is unfortunate since it is the right that should have been most carefully protected and enhanced.

8

The Tragedy: The Unplanned Consequence of Mind Control

"If you are to win an unfair game, you must find a better way to cheat."

—MAYER AMSCHEL ROTHSCHILD IN 1783, FRANKFURT, GERMANY

THE FRAMERS OF our Constitution used language that was clear at the time, but over the past two hundred years, the meanings of words have changed in ways that have actually changed the principles the founders intended. People no longer have the power that they were given at the time our government was organized. Justice increased in our society for the first hundred or so years, but that trend seems to have stalled. These two principles are still the core of our society, but their meanings have changed. People power and justice were the two foundations of our society; the people and the press were given the responsibility to protect society. Before and during the time that our Constitution was being developed, there was much discussion about the importance of responsible citizenship. The main phrase to describe that responsibility was that a good citizen needed to be honestly "informed and vigilant." What happened?

Completely answering that question in a complex society is impossible, but we can find a major cause of the tragedy when we look back at what our founders learned from the failures of the Romans and Greeks. Roman and Greek leaders believed that they structured their societies so that undo concentration of power, which is the greatest risk to a just society, was prevented. Sadly, those with greed for power in the society slowly adjusted the rules and principles so that concentration of power took place. It was two thousand years later that first Baron Acton in England wrote the now-universally accepted rule, "Power corrupts. Absolute power corrupts absolutely." It's possible that the rule is stated too strongly and should be, "Power *almost always* corrupts. Absolute power *almost always* corrupts absolutely," but that doesn't take away from the idea that concentration of power corrupts. When power is taken away from the people and given to a few, a just society suffers.

That's all well and good, but that shouldn't happen in the United States where the people are passionate about making our society *more perfect*. So there must be some great force for evil causing our failure. When we wake up from our reverie, that great force becomes apparent.

The historian-philosopher Frederick Nietzsche wrote, in the 1800s, what is now an almost-universally accepted rule, paraphrased, "there is no untruth that if repeated often enough and loud enough does not become the truth." This statement is hard to find in Nietzsche's published writings, but the idea has been repeated by many respected authors, stated more simply as "a lie told often enough and loud enough becomes the truth in the listener's mind." This is the basis for the powerful mind-control system called propaganda.

Propaganda hadn't been made into a powerful mind-control tool until Adolf Hitler came into power in Germany. Hitler appointed an enthusiastic student of Nietzsche's ideas—Adolph Goebels Reich Minister for Propaganda—who Hitler used to influence a high percentage of the otherwise civilized German public to bring Hitler to power. It was this use of propaganda that caused the Germans to believe in uncivilized actions, such as the Holocaust. Propaganda (mind control) made Hitler a veritable god among the Third Reich–leaning Germans. Goebbels was given complete control of radio, press, cinema, and theater in Germany, to effectively repeat lies often and loudly.

The world learned about the dangers of open propaganda after the lessons learned in Germany, so the users of propaganda went underground. The system was perfected so that it could sneak up on people. A number of hidden strategies were added to the base strategy of outright lie. The most effective strategies are now called *spin* and *labeling*. Spin is the strategy of adding some bit of truth to a lie, which makes the listener mistakenly believe that it is all true. This can be countered by the now-accepted saying, "part truths are all lie." Labeling is the propaganda strategy where naming something bad with a good name—containing such words as *freedom, free, liberty,* and a number of other good words—can make something bad suddenly good. This is another way to use propaganda to make a lie seem to be the truth. We now use propaganda as much of the basis for the science of marketing.

Propaganda (i.e., marketing, or mind control) has become a major force in both macro and the Main Street economies by changing the way competition is maintained as a controller of monopoly. Monopoly is primarily the effect of power concentration in the economy. Marketing has become increasingly important, impacting the way products and services are chosen. The use of propaganda as a mind-control strategy in commerce has been increasing for at least one hundred years, but has become many-times-more powerful since the arrival of television. Now, it is the amount and quality of marketing through advertising that determines the success and monopoly power of a product or service. This means that marketing creates much of the market-disrupting loss of competition in the marketplace. The mind-control effect of marketing often causes consumers to purchase unnecessary or even harmful products, such as expensive entertainment instead of education for their children, as one example. In that case, mind-controlled improper choices hurt the children, but also everyone else.

The most tragic effects of propaganda are that it firmly places improper ideas in a person's mind that work against the person's best interest, and it gives an advantage to those wanting control. These ideas become so embedded that the person follows directions given by the propagandist, almost like a robot. Thus, this is very effective in the marketing of ideas. This makes it very difficult for citizens to carry out their responsibility to be correctly *informed and vigilant*, thus the citizens fail to protect their *more perfect* society and government. In addition, the power of mind-controlling propaganda makes it difficult for the people to make corrections to injustices through the political process.

Since our founders had no way of predicting the problem of propaganda, they wrote the First Amendment to the Constitution in a way that protects without reservation the use of propaganda in our society. The US Supreme Court in the early 2000s had an opportunity to interpret the meaning of the First Amendment in a way that would limit the problem of propaganda, but the court was concerned that any adjustment to the interpretation of the First Amendment could have the unplanned consequence of limiting some of the protection intended in the amendment. Instead, they added an interpretation that strengthened the right of powerful interests to use unlimited propaganda. Therefore, we need to find some other means of controlling propaganda so that it can't weaken our ability to be *informed and vigilant*; the results of not doing so would damage our society's ability to remain a truly democratic republic.

Since the mid-twentieth century, messages of propaganda have been coupled with messages of hate. This started mostly on the radio, but it became more common and effective with the advent of television. These messages seem to

elicit a strong fascination for humans—that continuously lis-
tening to and watching such broadcasts seems to become an
addiction. This addiction makes it difficult or impossible for
citizens to rationally consider issues that are necessary for
their being informed and vigilant on the issues of our society. These people who are influenced by propaganda tend to
become vigorous participants in the decision-making process;
therefore, the uninfluenced people need to protect their
freedom by also vigorously participating in the process of citizenship. They not only need to vote, but also, to the best of
their abilities, find the truth so they can be informed and vigilant in order to make a well-considered vote. It is also part of
the responsibility of citizenship to help others to be properly
informed and vigilant.

In recent years, a more insidious and unplanned effect
of propaganda is that, as more and more people have come
under the mind-control power of propaganda, this has
allowed the chain reaction of *groupthink* to take place. People
who have not yet been controlled see their trusted friends
and family members believing propaganda falsehoods, causing them to more easily fall under the spell. Their friends are
similarly influenced, and a chain reaction starts that can affect
an entire population.

Since living with propaganda has become unavoidable, we
need to find some way to thwart its power. We may find the
power when we look at people who seem to be immune to
the effect of mind control. These people have learned to be
informed and vigilant, as our founders requested. They are
rigid about looking for the real truth in the information they

receive and, by force of will, avoid believing propaganda. This likely wouldn't apply to a large population unless the skill was taught to children early in their education. In the meantime, we can just hope that our society can survive this destructive influence.

9

Taxes: Loved and Hated

"The subjects of every state ought to contribute toward the support of the government, as nearly as possible, in proportion to their respective abilities."

—Adam Smith, *Wealth of Nations*

ARE TAXES GOOD or bad, compared with the other purchases we make? Are there other reasons for taxes besides government purchases of goods and services? These are good questions, and the answers to both are yes and no.

Taxes are good when they pay for goods and services the public needs, and the public seriously needs most of the services our taxes provide. We sometimes need taxes to help establish justice when it is threatened by overconcentration of wealth and power, which has grown because of insufficient competition. One example of such a tax is the graduated income tax where the wealthy pay at a higher rate to compensate for the inequality of wealth and power. For this purpose, the income tax affects only income and not total wealth. Total wealth is only affected at the time of death by the estate tax, which at this time is very low. Equality can also be strengthened by keeping lower taxes on products and services that are more commonly purchased by the middle and lower class. These taxes are usually sales and income taxes. The graduated income tax and estate tax are higher for those who have been able to concentrate wealth, thus contributing to equality of opportunity. If competition is working to justly control the market, it would be difficult to concentrate wealth and power that limits equality of opportunity, thus the estate tax would not be needed.

We sometimes fail to appreciate the benefits we get from jointly funding, through taxation, the safety net provided by the police and military, the education system, the firefighting system, the justice system, the welfare system for the needy, the transportation system, infrastructure, and many others. Tax money spent on that class of services is probably as important or possibly more important than many of a citizen's personal expenditures in the regular economy. Taxes benefit society the most when the money is spent where it can return to the flow. For example, most of the tax money paid to teachers, police, and firefighters will be spent in the Main Street economy and returned to the flow.

Much of the tax money spent for military equipment and money given to foreign countries will be moved to the macro economy, becoming leakage from the flow. This leakage doesn't seriously hurt the economy if there is enough new money coming into the flow to keep the flow strong and to continue the high velocity of money movement.

We have had an income tax for over a hundred years, but in the early 1900s, it was challenged in the Supreme Court and was partially deemed unconstitutional. The Sixteenth Amendment, ratified in 1913, made the income tax permanent with the rates to be set yearly by Congress. The Depression of the early 1930s seems to not affect the very wealthy, but it left the majority of the population in poverty—and that majority was outraged. President Franklin Roosevelt was very concerned about the problem and urged Congress to set a very high graduated-income tax rate. The result was called the *Soak the Rich* tax; the 1935 rate went to 75 percent on the very wealthy. The rate of one person, John D. Rockefeller, went to 79 percent on his income of five million, which would be about eighty-five million today. Rockefeller said in a speech that he thought the tax was very fair. Later in the twentieth century, the rate went as high as 91 percent. The very wealthy were angered, and they worked and lobbied to get the rate cut to about 25 percent at one time. The top rate in 2014 was 39.6 percent, which applied to the top 1 percent. The problem with the graduated income tax is that it is riddled with loopholes. Some very wealthy—with good tax accountants and lawyers—have been able, in years past, to reduce their tax to zero while most middle-class taxpayers have been required to pay full tax rates on their total income after deductions. The investor class and more-well-off taxpayers have been able to take advantage of special tax rates on dividends, capital gains, and special depreciation advantages. These are not loopholes, but they are normal tax rules, and most of these rules have been put in place by the work of lobbyists acting to benefit those with special interests.

The estate tax and inheritance tax are the best taxes for maintaining total wealth equality, but they are fought by the wealthy as vigorously as they battle the graduated income tax. State inheritance taxes have been almost entirely removed. In 2001, federal estate tax on estates of less than $675,000 were exempt, and the rate over that was 55 percent. In 2014, the top estate tax rate applied to estates of over $5.34 million and the maximum rate was 40 percent. The exempted amount will continue to go up, and the rate will continue to go down until it eventually reaches zero. To be effective in producing wealth equality, the base exemption could be several million dollars, but the rate would need to be very high with no other exemptions beyond the base exemption, and it should cover wealth earned or moved out of the country by citizens, non-citizens, or nonresidents. Such rules would probably require an amendment to the Constitution.

We have always had as a principle of our society that Americans should maintain equality of opportunity, by believing people should be able to gain wealth and power only through individual initiative, rather than through circumstances of birth.

The feeling in most American families is that parents should give their children as much education and training advantages as possible and also, if necessary, support them with loans to fund entrepreneurial ventures.

Many have used their wealth and power to elect friendly people to Congress and to lobby Congress in creating unfair laws concerning most taxes. This was at one time a small problem, but in recent years, the problem has become a serious violation of our core principles.

10

Banking, Interest Rates, and Fun

MONOPOLY, AS IN the Monopoly game, makes extreme profits a possibility, which is fun. Making extreme profits on money that is often not even owned by the player, like the banks sometimes do, is even greater fun.

Traditionally, banks pay their expenses and earn their profits on the interest spread between the amount they pay depositors and the amount they earn on loans. The spread pays the expenses of the bank, such as salaries of employees, and the reasonable profits to the owners. The amount of profit was traditionally kept reasonable by competition from other banks and by fair rules. This traditional type of banking was a great benefit to society because people could save money for future use, such as retirement, by depositing it in the bank to collect interest. The banks could then loan the money back to individuals and businesses that would spend it back into the Main Street economy. That was much better than people just putting money into a safe, which would stop the flow until the money was eventually spent. Banks were required to keep part of their money in reserve to pay depositors who wanted to withdraw their funds. Banks were at risk because bad economic news or another bank offering higher interest rates could cause a *run* on the bank, causing people to withdraw more money than the bank held in reserve for payouts. The government developed an insurance system to prevent bank failures due to runs, making banks, over the years, safe and stable places for people to keep their savings.

In the past hundred years or so, banks have changed. Many are no longer the simple savings-and-loan organizations that they traditionally were. Many banks still operate in the Main Street economy. Now the big banks function almost entirely in the macro economy, and the average person has little understanding of how macro banking works, but they are suspicious that it is not in their best interest. Part of the problem has come about because the Federal Reserve controls the money supply, thus it is essentially banking-industry controlled. The Federal Reserve Bank has the ability to create money and give it value; therefore, the banks themselves can decide how much money is created. The created money supply needs to be regulated, and the banks have usually carried out that responsibility fairly. In recent years, there has been a large concentration of money going into the macro economy, which leaves the country at risk of drastic hyperinflation if this money was to be moved into the Main Street economy too quickly. This problem has been partly caused by congressional action. The Federal Reserve isn't entirely to blame.

The Fed (the Federal Reserve Bank) creates the money and loans it to banks at an extremely low-interest rate. The banks then loan it to whomever can use it to stimulate the economy. The spread, the difference between the Fed loan rate and the bank loan rate, isn't great, but when it involves trillions of dollars, the potential profit is astronomical. And the money isn't actually theirs—it's the people's, who are on the hook for backing it. The trouble is that often there is little demand for bank money to stimulate the economy in a good way, so banks look for ways to do it in a bad way. They are required by rules to loan to people who are proven to be capable of repayment, but banks have been known to weaken the rules to loan large amounts to millions of people to buy expensive homes without reasonable ability to pay. These loans also required fees, sometimes sizable fees, that had significant impacts on the banks' bottom lines. The system was a bubble that would obviously burst, so many of the homes were repossessed by the banks.,. There are questions about what happened at this point, but apparently the banks had to make some repayments, requiring a "bailout of the banks." This bailout was carried out by the Fed creating several trillions more dollars of the people's money and loaning it to the banks. Somehow, late in that time, the big banks reported record-breaking profits.

It's interesting that during 2007 and 2008, I lived in a small town and often had morning coffee at the drugstore with a small group of very ordinary people. One morning, one of the members reported being concerned because his friend, a waitress who had saved enough money for a small down payment, was able to receive a loan for well over one hundred thousand dollars for a home. The starter payments at that time weren't high, and the loan salesman assured her she had nothing to worry about, even though the interest rate and payments were scheduled to become higher after a short time. When the waitress found that she had agreed to a loan where the interest and the payment could be increased after a time, and she was already getting behind on her payments. She lost the house, her savings, and most importantly her feelings of being in control, or as we said at one time, her pursuit of happiness.

We at the drugstore were sure, though most had no financial training, that there was going to be a crash, as this case was not isolated but rather characteristic of what was happening. It was even more interesting that, after the crash happened, the big bankers said there was no way they could have predicted the crash, with many in Congress believing them. But those ordinary, untrained people sitting around the table in the drugstore were able to predict this. For millions of people, the crash caused a devastating recession. For the big bankers, it was fun—just like it was fun for one person to gain a monopoly in the family Monopoly game and wipe out the rest of us.

After the crash, some in Congress tried to develop new rules to prevent this from ever happening again. The banks were opposed. Getting congressional approval of any rule was difficult, and the law that finally came out was weak, and even that law was further weakened. I still have coffee at the drugstore sometimes and visit with people. Now, the concern is about people wanting big and expensive pickup trucks, and they are common vehicles on the streets in this area. One of the people sitting at the drugstore table recently told about his friend who had just purchased a pickup truck for over fifty thousand dollars. The small down payment was covered by the trade-in of his old truck, which had little value. This person, like the waitress mentioned earlier, has low or zero savings, yet he was able to get a loan for almost the entire amount. The person at the drugstore had tried to counsel the person not to buy the truck because the costs could be a real problem for his family. The truck buyer said he was going to go ahead because he wanted it badly even though the final cost—including interest, if he was able to keep the truck—would be approximately ninety thousand dollars. Are people around the country once again going into debt to buy trucks, SUVs, and cars with easy money borrowed from the banks? If so, is it happening again?

People in Congress need to understand that weak banking laws lead to great injustices. The people still have a vote, but they must use their vote effectively. During the congressional consideration of banking laws following the great recession, one prominent Senator was asked about how the work was going. He said that some legislators were trying hard to pass a good law, "but we have to face it, the banks own this place."

11

Basic Economics on the Personal Level

PUBLIC INFORMATION ABOUT economics arrives engulfed in a giant smokescreen. There are many beliefs about how economics operates, but many are beliefs that are manufactured to further some person's or group's personal or greed-based interest. This leads to confusion in the mind of a person trying to gain an honest understanding of the science, or some say pseudoscience. There is an old saying that "the science of economics makes astrology seem scientific." I relate that kiddingly since I have a brother that is a well-known and respected economist, one that was at one time on the economic advisory staff of President Kennedy.

Economics is understandable and scientific when learned through the very basic teachings of Adam Smith, and others from the 18th century, and John Maynard Keynes, and others from the nineteenth and twentieth centuries. In addition, the best way to understand economics is to actually live through and be observant of the upturns and downturns during one of the most instructive hundred years in history. That can be done by following one average middle-class family through those years.

This story starts in the last years of the nineteenth century, which is considered the starting time for modern economics. Theodore Roosevelt was just ending his presidency, a time when the trusts had been dismantled and the monopolies—created by the robber barons—had just been broken up; money was returning to the Main Street economy, and dollars were beginning to flow. This was ending a recession caused by the immense concentration of wealth and power by a few wealthy people.

The young family of four lived in Illinois, and they were quickly recovering from the downturn because the father was an electrical engineer and had advanced into a good job for a major railroad. His job was designing signal systems to prevent rail crashes, which resulted in the invention of semaphore signals that are still in use on some railroads. This accomplishment led to him becoming chief electrical engineer for the railroad. Even though it was improving, the flow of money on Main Street was still low because the flow at that time came largely from the wages of manufacturing and other industrial labor. The monopolists were still powerful enough to keep labor pay extremely low, but the organized labor movement was starting.

The father, my grandfather, understood economics and the importance of money flow, and he realized that raising wages was the only practical way to increase Main Street flow of money. He was sympathetic to the men in his department when they wanted a union to increase their income. Management wasn't sympathetic, so my grandfather was fired and blackballed. Being blackballed was an agreement between managers in major industries, which meant that the person could not be hired in any industry, subject to the agreement for any major job. The only good option left was finding an opportunity to enter the market by becoming an entrepreneur.

Two railroads had built lines through Montana to the Pacific Northwest in the early 1900s, and under a government stimulus program at the time, the railroads were given large tracts of land on both sides of the tracks. In western Montana, the lines ran through heavily timbered mountains that, in 1910, suffered the largest forest fire in American history. It included much of the Canadian central mountains, the mountains of west-central South Dakota, all the mountains of western Montana, all of northern Idaho above the Salmon River, and parts of eastern Washington. It became known in history as the Big Burn, and the smoke made it necessary to keep lights on in the daytime in Chicago and New York; the ash blackened the ice of Greenland. This made all the timber—as owned by the railroads in the area—dead and black from the fire, so the railroad management decided that its land was now nearly worthless.

My grandparents had some savings and the desire to become pioneers out West. They knew about the fire and felt that there surely must be some use for all the black timber. They went west, and with their small amount of money, they were able to buy about two thousand acres of mountains and black trees. The property was near the Montana-Idaho border. The railroad ran through the property, over the Bitterroot Divide, and into the silver-mining area known as Silver Valley. Silver Valley had been burned during the fire, but it had recovered by 1912 with major expansions of the mines. Mine tunnels are shored up by heavy posts and cross-logs arranged along the ceilings. But mines are wet, and the logs tended to rot. It was discovered that black, burned logs were very resistant to rot, so suddenly there was a good market for black logs cut into mine timbers. Since the railroad could deliver the timbers, the family was in business. The blackball hadn't followed my grandfather out West, so he was able to get a job maintaining the signals on the railroad through the mountains; thus, he wasn't available for the timber business, but he had two young sons—my eventual father who was sixteen, and his younger brother who was fifteen. The two of them cut the trees, loaded the trees on a wagon with a horse-powered derrick, hauled them to the railroad, and loaded them on flat cars with another horse-powered derrick. It was a good business, which was fortunate because there were now several more younger brothers and sisters.

The area by the railroad that they eventually called the ranch became a little community that had a one-room school. My grandfather was chairman of the school board and was responsible for hiring the teacher. She came by train from Spokane, arriving in the evening. My grandfather sent his son, later my father, to meet her at the train. In later years, I called her Mom. Mom, Dad, and I later left the ranch and moved to Portland where he attended a trade school to become an industrial electrician. He already knew much of it from working with his dad on the signals. He worked for the electric power utility in Washington for several years, finally buying acreage in Spokane Valley for our home—and then the Great Depression started. The utility didn't lay off its employees, but it cut back on their time. In fact, my father was cut back to one day a month, and he was lucky compared to many workers in the Spokane area. Poverty became so severe that you could see it, feel it, and almost taste it. We had the acreage and a cow, so we could raise our own food and keep some of our friends' families from malnutrition with our surplus.

The only means of communication with the outside world was the newfangled radio that some fortunately owned before the Depression. For the first two or three years, there was no good news. The president would speak on the radio, promising that there soon would be "a chicken in every pot," but it was only an unfulfilled hope. The government was trying to save us by stimulating production so that people could buy the products that would increase demand and start the flow of money. The government economists said that starting production would require hiring employees, thus providing money for the flow. However, companies had little money to start production, and if they did, there were few buyers because the people had little money. It was obvious to most of the people, but not to the government, that getting money to the people would have to come before production could start. The government was using *supply first* economics. But most of the people knew that demand for goods and services happened through people having money to make purchases, which would stimulate supply, thus people would need to be hired to manufacture that supply, making the economic recovery self-stimulating. We had to use *demand first* economics. In a depression, there is no good way for the private sector to get money to the people to create demand, thus making it possible for them to buy things; therefore, the government, somehow, would need to provide the money to start the flow. We were stuck and frightened. There was nothing we could do. President Herbert Hoover was a good man, but he believed strongly in questionable economics. He began to change his thinking during the last few months of his administration, and he proposed borrowing money to build a huge dam in the West, Boulder Dam, to create construction jobs and get some money flowing.

I was still a child, but I can remember people talking about economics and about the fact that bad economic policy had caused the miseries that we were experiencing. Everybody talked about it, with most blaming the fact that vast amounts of money had gone up to the macro economy, the economy of the extremely wealthy, so there was little left to flow on Main Street. It was the third and darkest year of the Depression when the presidential election campaign started. It was the first time that radio was heavily used in a campaign, and Franklin Roosevelt used it a lot. He talked about his plan to start money flowing in order to break the grip of the Depression. His plan was to accomplish two things: one was to borrow the money, even if it was provided at a higher interest rate, in order to get it spread out to the people around the country; and his second planned accomplishment was to break the grip of fear in the population, because it's true that economic depression causes mental depression. The economic depression was causing a serious increase in suicide—and starvation was beginning to occur. Living through that, as my mother used to say, "gets your head cut in."

Sadly, the people of the generation who lived through the Great Depression and the war and who participated in rebuilding America after those troubled times failed to pass on the wisdom gained during those difficult times to the generations that followed.

The actions of the new administration by 1937 reduced the Depression to a recession. In one effective action, President Roosevelt led Congress to move the United States off the gold standard, which had required all currency to be backed by an equal amount of gold. The gold standard had limited the availability of money to the amount of gold stored at Fort Knox. Removing that requirement made it possible for the government, through the new Federal Reserve, to create money based on the faith and credit of the people, so it was easier to move money into the flow without having to borrow at high-interest rates, if available at all. Unfortunately, the new money had to go through the big banks and had to be treated as loans to the Treasury as making the new-money debt, and this all was very profitable to the banks and investors who bought the bonds (as it still is).

My father got his first full-time job in several years in 1936, working on the Grand Coulee Dam. Many were still unemployed, but the severe poverty was lessening. The economic conditions of the family and everyone improved steadily through the next several decades until monopoly in the economy began to cause recessions, culminating in the great recessions of the 2000s.

12

The Political Economic System Is Lost, but Not Forever

"Liberty may be endangered by the abuse of liberty, but also by the abuse of power."

—James Madison

POLITICAL ECONOMICS IS the core of our livelihoods, our national safety, our domestic tranquility, and our general welfare, which are all objective principles of our Constitution. Yet, we can see that we have a political economy that is providing nearly the opposite of all those things for a high percentage of our population.

We have been examining the political economic system from all sides, and it is self-evident that the power that was intended for the people has been concentrated into the hands of a few. Great power is no longer the product of great violence and wars. Now, great power is more commonly produced by great wealth. It is now easier and better to buy power than to steal it with violence.

Some say power is good, and it would be better if we had a powerful ruler to eliminate bickering and controversy. "Kings and other monarchs are good" has been the universal opinion of people over the millennia, but that would require a benevolent monarch like King Arthur of Camelot. Wait—that was legend. Mahatma Gandhi of India is very likely the only real person in history who could have qualified, but he was not a monarch.

Our founders believed, and now the majority of Americans believe, that a republic where the power is with the people is the best form of society, and concentration of power is society's greatest danger. When that concentration of power is based on great wealth, it leads to the purchasing of laws that provides the resources to do such things as create monopolies, one of the destroyers of a just political economy. The most insidious use of wealth is in the purchase of people's minds through propaganda, using our immense media system, which is very expensive but extremely effective. This makes it difficult for citizens to use honest data to monitor the activities of their government and society, which in turn robs people of their rightful power under the Constitution to be *We the People* in control of the nation.

If the people weren't unduly influenced by propaganda and its corollary groupthink, we could change our laws and even some bits of the Constitution to re-create a fair political economy based on competition and rules of fair play. This would make it impossible to concentrate power through wealth. The people, being informed and vigilant, would give us the *more perfect* society that was the objective of our founders when they decided to clearly state the basic and firm principles that would be the foundation of our new country in the first sentence of the Constitution.

www.ingramcontent.com/pod-product-compliance
Lightning Source LLC
Chambersburg PA
CBHW070818180526
45168CB00002B/659